Natural-Born Soulmates

Follow Your Inner Wisdom to Lasting Love

Lauren Thibodeau, Ph.D.

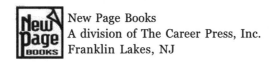
New Page Books
A division of The Career Press, Inc.
Franklin Lakes, NJ

NATURAL-BORN SOULMATES
EDITED BY KATHRYN HENCHES
TYPESET BY MICHAEL FITZGIBBON
Cover design by Leeza Hernandez/Conker Tree
Printed in the U.S.A. by Book-mart Press

To order this title, please call toll-free 1-800-CAREER-1 (NJ and Canada: 201-
848-0310) to order using VISA or MasterCard, or for further information on books
from Career Press.

The Career Press, Inc., 3 Tice Road, PO Box 687,
Franklin Lakes, NJ 07417
www.careerpress.com
www.newpagebooks.com

Library of Congress Cataloging-in-Publication Data
Thibodeau, Lauren.
    Natural-born soulmates : follow your inner wisdom to lasting love / by Lauren
Thibodeau.
        p. cm.
    ISBN-13:978-1-56414-928-2
    ISBN-10: 1-56414-928-5
    1. Soul mates. I. Title.

BF1045.I58T48 2007
158.2—dc22

                                                                    2007019579

DEDICATION

Natural-Born Soulmates is dedicated to all those who believe in the power of love, but especially to my husband and Heartmate of more than 20 years, Ed, who believes in me and who shows me every day just how much.

Acknowledgments

Many people assisted me in the process of writing *Natural-Born Soulmates* but a few of my soulmates, treasured friends, and colleagues deserve special mention.

Canadian friend, Maria D., was supportive throughout the project, providing helpful insights, joyful interruptions when I needed them, and entertaining tales of dating in Toronto. She kept me on task during a time when life kept me frazzled, and delighted me by popping on a split of Champagne to share a toast by telephone when the project was completed. Mille grazie, dear Maria D.

Brilliant photographer and friend, Shannon Taggart, provided another author photo (as she did for *Natural-Born Intuition*), plus prints of some of her terrific work to adorn my office, including powerful images of my students and me. A story-teller with words as well as photos, Shannon kept me laughing over diner food at the corner place near my office—and she gifted me with a Starbucks card for which she earns bonus points. Visit *ShannonTaggart.com* and you'll see for yourself why my intuition tells me fame is in her future. Thank you, my friend and traveling buddy.

I'd also like to thank my mediumship students who kept me focused and, more importantly, kept me centered throughout the writing process. The vibes we generate together lift me up, and remind me why I teach. If you've ever believed that spiritual people can't live in large cities, I assure you, they can and they do. The transformations they ignite, simply by being who they are, reach far beyond the city limits.

Joëlle Delbourgo and Molly Lyons offered not only the great gift of becoming (and remaining) an author, they were unfailingly supportive and appropriately nudge-y when life threw a few curves my way during the course of this project. Thank you both for your professionalism, your patience, and your prodding.

Finally a special thank you goes to senior editor Michael Pye and the rest of the staff at Career Press/New Page books for their ongoing support of my work. Without them, you wouldn't be holding this book right now.

Contents

Preface

In *Natural-Born Soulmates: Follow Your Inner Wisdom to Lasting Love,* I continue my goal of helping you to access and apply your Inner Wisdom, which was the focus of my first book, *Natural-Born Intuition.* But this time, it's all about relationships. Family. Friends. Colleagues. Lovers. As you'll see, learning to work with your Inner Wisdom can lead you to much improved, much happier, and much more fulfilling relationships. And if it's romance you're interested in (and really, who isn't?), *Natural-Born Soulmates* provides practical principles that can help you transform your current relationship, or attract new romantic opportunities.

Throughout the book I refer to romantic soulmates as Heartmates. Other style conventions include the premise that Heartmate relationships are between male and female partners, and that the reader is female. Please know that the information is equally applicable to male readers seeking female partners, as well as to same- gender romantic relationships. And although I am well aware that not everyone is seeking a marriage or domestic partnership, to avoid cumbersome phrases in the text, I sometimes use the term *marriage* when the context could also be a long-term, living-together relationship, or a longstanding romantic relationship with partners who do not live together.

Because most people are most comfortable focusing on creating a deeper connection within one sexually intimate relationship at a time, *Natural-Born Soulmates* is written with the goal of improving or attracting a monogamous relationship in mind. Still, the concepts presented can be applied if you are involved in more than one romantic connection simultaneously. In fact, in such a case, *Natural-Born Soulmates* may be invaluable in helping you to decide which, if any, of your current romantic liaisons have Heartmate potential.

The modern convention is to use "someone" paired with "their" when grammatically "someone" and "his or her" is the more traditional usage. To avoid cumbersome phrasing, I have used the modern convention throughout *Natural-Born Soulmates*.

As you work with what I call your Personal Resonance—that unique soul-level vibe that sets you apart from everyone else—in your relationships, I welcome your feedback about your successes (and yes, even your struggles) in applying the techniques outlined in *Natural-Born Soulmates*. Visit my Website, *DrLauren.com*, to share your story.

And as you reach to your Inner Wisdom, please know that I'm honored to assist you in learning to access that still, small voice, the wisdom within, the call of your Soul.

Introduction:
The Soulmate Path

Love doesn't make the world go 'round. Love is what makes the ride worthwhile.

—Franklin P. Jones

You've picked this book up for a reason: You're ready to take on the challenges and especially the rewards of soulmate relationships, to walk along what I call the Soulmate Path. If you're ready for the adventure, I'm ready to help you learn to access and, more importantly, apply your Inner Wisdom—the voice of your soul—to the process of attracting the kind of relationships that fulfill you body, mind, spirit, and, of course, soul.

In *Natural-Born Soulmates*, you'll learn about what I call your Personal Resonance: the unique and special soul vibration that's yours alone. By working with your Personal Resonance and your Inner Wisdom or Inner Soulmate, you can be guided to powerful, productive partnerships with soulmates of all types. That includes the special kind of romantic soulmate relationship which I call a Heartmate bond that you may have thought was impossible for you.

You'll also learn about two other important categories of soulmates: Karmic Connections and Balance Partners. Even if you think your life is rife with challenging people (none of whom you can see as a soulmate), you'll find that Karmic Connections (people with whom you have soul-level unfinished business) can be nurtured into Balance Partners (people who provide support and encouragement as you maneuver along the Soulmate Path). And from there, you can even grow into Heartmates. So, whether you're seeking a new romantic soulmate relationship, or want to transform the one you're in now, *Natural-Born Soulmates* teaches you to use the power of your own being, your own soul essence, that powerful Personal Resonance to attract what you want in your relationships. That includes family members, friends, and school and business associates, too.

Through managing your Personal Resonance, your vibrational PR, you will become what I call spiritually efficient. Spiritual efficiency derives from clear intentions about what you want to accomplish in your relationships. It sweeps away the clutter and reduces the scatter, allowing you to broadcast your Personal Resonance more effectively. Often spiritual efficiency leaves what feels like chaos in its wake, but you can't begin to fill up a space with new things until you've cleared out the old clutter. Keep in mind that chaos preceded order from the very beginning.

As you read, please remind yourself that change is a constant. Change is inevitable. Change is natural. Change is life—that flowing river. Releasing your fears about change is an important step as you embark on the Soulmate Path, and nearly all blocks in your Personal Resonance can be traced back to fear of change in some form. You don't have to embrace change with the glee of a 4-year-old excited to play outside on a summer day, but you must learn to accept change. You need to be flexible if you want to see transformed existing soulmate and Heartmate relationships, or to attract new ones.

Think about why you're reading this book. What patterns in your relationships do you want to see transformed? What are you willing to do to achieve that transformation? How serious are you about really getting the most from your relationships with family members, friends, colleagues, and lovers? At this point you may find it helpful to write down your concerns about changes in your life. This will help you begin to relax into that ride along the river of life, where every moment things are different from even just a moment ago.

Fear of change is the most challenging aspect of transforming relationships for most people. But fear is a form of Personal Resonance. It transmits. And it attracts on the same vibe about which you can later say (from the level of your ego rather than your soul),

"See? I told you so. Change is a bad thing." You get to be right on an ego level. But wouldn't you rather be happy in a deeper way, on the level of your soul?

Bottom line: Powerful, positive soulmate and Heartmate connections begin with *you*. Through *Natural-Born Soulmates* I want to help you attract and enjoy the kind of relationships that leave you feeling that life simply couldn't be any better. I want to help you understand that working on your own soul and development is the key to attract soulmates. Rewarding, trustful, and joyful relationships. And yes, romantic Heartmate bonds, too.

The Focus Factor

As with anything in life that you're passionate about, focus is important to accomplishment. That includes attracting soulmates and Heartmates into your life to shift your relationship playing ground to a better place. The focus factor will help you become much better at accessing and applying your Inner Wisdom. With disciplined focus, a regular practice of tuning into your Inner Wisdom, your Personal Resonance can become so efficient that the results may astonish you. What took months or years to manifest in your life may now take only days or weeks. That's what this whole book is about, actually: how attending to your personal growth and spiritual development changes your Personal Resonance—your vibe—which transforms everything.

This spiritual development process can be accelerated, and the river rapids along the way minimized, with the ongoing assistance of your Inner Wisdom, which you may prefer to think of as a kind of Inner Soulmate. Throughout the book, I'll use both terms interchangeably. If you prefer to have a name and identity associated with insights and messages from your Inner Wisdom, go ahead: Name your angel or spirit guide. Many people find just trusting the Source, God, the Infinite Intelligence, or the Field is enough (especially those of us who can't remember names anyway). Do what feels comfortable to you because the more relaxed you are in this process, the better and faster it will work.

Whatever you term your Inner Wisdom, your source of spiritual guidance, know this: It's designed to help you in your soul development. That's its prime directive, to borrow a term from science fiction.

You may wish to take a moment now to close your eyes, relax a bit, and ask for a name to use when you request guidance from your Inner Wisdom, for a name to use to reach for that Inner Soulmate. If you receive a name or an image, color, or symbol associated with your Inner Soulmate, that's fine. And if not, that's fine too: Just allow the process of inquiry and connection to begin.

A Few Simple Rules

There's really no big mystery to the process of attracting soulmates, which include Karmic Connections, Balance Partners, and Heartmates. Following your Inner Wisdom to lasting love boils down to a few simple rules:

1. Ask your Inner Wisdom for guidance.
2. Follow it.

A big issue for many people is discerning when they're dealing with the voice of their Inner Wisdom or their own beliefs, hopes or fears. Mental chatter is something with which all human beings live. Clearing that mental clutter so you can better discern what your Inner Wisdom is guiding you toward is an ongoing challenge. Synchronicities, those meaningful coincidences that serve as directional signs along the Soulmate Path, are important to note. Dreams also carry powerful insights about our lives. And trusting your perceptions and feelings matters, too.

Even what seem to be random thoughts that arrive out of nowhere are important. These are often signs from your Inner Wisdom, not your thinking mind. Remember that thinking takes time, focus, and discipline. To ponder. To mull over. To ruminate. All those synonyms for thinking point out that thinking sounds like hard work. It takes effort.

So the effortless feeling of an idea or insight just popping into your head is suggestive of your Inner Wisdom, not your thinking mind, at work. As you read *Natural-Born Soulmates* I encourage you to start a journal, blog, audio or video file, or other record of signs and synchronicities you receive. You'll find it helpful later in assessing your progress and negotiating that river of life and the Soulmate Path.

Even if you can't quite hear that inner voice yet, rest assured that you are not walking down the Soulmate Path alone, even when it feels that way. Your Inner Wisdom always walks along with you. Your Inner Soulmate has always got your back. You just need to learn how to listen to that powerful Inner Wisdom, how to discern guidance from goals, wisdom from wanting.

Throughout this book, I'll introduce you to many other new ideas, too. These include the three major categories of what I call your Outer Soulmates (as compared to your Inner Soulmate/Inner Wisdom): Karmic Connections, Balance Partners, and Heartmate Bonds. Any one—probably every one—of these categories of soulmate can be found somewhere in your life at any given time. You may find a Karmic Connection soulmate within your family, a few Balance Partner Soulmates within the workplace, and a potential Heartmate Bond connection in a chance encounter on an airplane. I'll address each of those types of soulmate connections in future chapters.

I'll also introduce you to what I call the Five Big Blocks when it comes to soulmate relationships, particularly romantic ones or those with Heartmate bond potential. Chapter 7 begins the journey to discovering how you're getting in the way of your own relationship success. What I call the Five Big Lessons are also important because every soulmate you encounter will have at least one of these five core interactions woven into the tapestry of your relationship with him or her. Having a sense of the Big Lesson you're dealing with is like having an advance look at the lesson plan for a class you're considering taking: it makes successful learning much, much easier. The Five Big Lessons are Passion, Purpose, Potential, Pacing, and Problem Solving, which we'll discuss in more detail beginning with Chapter 11.

Understanding the blocks and lessons you may not (yet) be consciously aware of will help you strategize the best ways to get the most out of your interactions with your soulmates: Karmic Connections, Balance Partners, and Heartmates, too. It's all about paying attention to your Personal Resonance, and using the power of your intention to change that vibe. You can exercise your free will in this very moment, Now to transform your viewpoint, which shifts your Personal Resonance, which in turn energizes the process of change in your life.

Right now, I suggest that you take a moment to assess whether you're truly emotionally and spiritually ready to work on attracting soulmates, particularly romantic ones (Heartmates), through working with your Personal Resonance. All deliberate changes you undertake, even those for the better, require adjustments to your life. If you are passionate about attracting enriching, fulfilling soulmate relationships, particularly Heartmates of the romantic variety, you'll need to put time and energy into the process for it to be the most effective.

If the timing for you to put the Soulmate Plan fully into action is off right now, acknowledge that. It's fine. Even small, consistent changes in your Personal Resonance eventually lead to big results. Taking more time to test out the process in small ways allows you to gain insight and awareness as you move toward bigger changes. Just remember that, as with anything else, the more you invest in the process, the better the results you'll achieve. So please, be realistic about how much time and energy you can invest in the soulmate journey at this time in your life. You don't want to end up feeling that somehow you didn't get it "right" when you simply lack time right now. Attracting soulmates, particularly a life partner or Heartmate, requires a greater investment of energy than attracting other types of soulmate connections such as new friendships. Yes, it sometimes seems that romantic soulmates just magically find each other and fall in love, but the truth is, that's the final step in a much longer journey, one that may even span lifetimes.

Whether you wish to start by creating small changes or big ones, keep reading: You will glean plenty of powerful insights about yourself and your Personal Resonance from *Natural-Born Soulmates* no matter what stage of the process you're in at this moment. And remember that your Inner Wisdom, that Inner Soulmate who wants you to live a joyous life within your relationships, will let you know when the time *is* right to put more energy into the Soulmate Path.

The Power of Belief

As you embark on the Soulmate Path, you will need to let go of some treasured beliefs, or at least suspend them for a while. Now is the ideal time to try out some new methods to achieve what you're looking for in your life. After all, if what you've been doing was working perfectly, you probably wouldn't be reading *Natural-Born Soulmates*. So it's definitely time to clear out the blocks to progress you may not even realize are there.

As you trace those long-held beliefs to their origins, and determine whether they still serve you now, many emotions are likely to surface. You may be surprised to uncover long-buried sadness or anger. As a result you may have to face your fears of being hurt (again) in love.

You may have to let go of long-held resentments toward others who caused you pain in the past. You also may need to heal your past of traumas, particularly those which have left deep emotional or even physical scars. You may need to forgive others, as a gift to yourself. You may discover that it's time to end some relationships of long standing, because they no longer resonate with who you are today. And, most importantly, you will need to forgive yourself, to let go of any guilt about choices you've made in past (and present) relationships. Forgiveness frees you. That's precisely why it's so powerful, and among the greatest gifts you can give yourself.

You may find you need time to digest some of the ideas I'll present in *Natural-Born Soulmates*. The concepts presented here are not ones you've seen before, which is why this book is likely to trigger fresh ideas and insightful responses in you as you react to this new information. For this reason, it's a very good idea to take things at a pace that works for you, and continually update that journal, blog, video, or audio file of your experiences as you read and respond to *Natural-Born Soulmates*. Your notes will be extremely helpful in understanding your Personal Resonance, that soul-level vibration that drives the entire process of attraction.

Remember: This book is designed for *you*, to help you learn about *you*, to help you understand how *your* Personal Resonance operates. It's always a good move to invest in yourself, in heightened self-awareness and greater self-love. That affects the quality of your Personal Resonance. The better the quality of your Personal Resonance, the better the quality of soulmate interaction opportunities you will attract. Sometimes stated in folk wisdom as "like attracts like" or "birds of a feather flock together" (and lately as "The Law of Attraction"), this is an entirely natural process over which you have a huge amount of influence. You may as well use that influence, that personal power derived from your Personal Resonance, to transform your life. But I encourage you to use to be smart about it, to be spiritually efficient. Why "work" harder than you have to?

Spiritual efficiency is the process of attaining the greatest spiritual output (soul-level learning) from any given input (life experience). Your soul's development benefits from learning and experience. In fact, that's exactly *how* your soul develops. By using the methods outlined in *Natural-Born Soulmates*, you're signing on for accelerated learning. You clearly want to get the most from your life when it comes to relationships.

Whether you want to heal and transform an existing romantic soulmate relationship or attract a new one, that powerful Heartmate relationship you long for can be yours. Welcome to the adventure. I'm honored to be your guide as you take your first steps along the Soulmate Path.

Chapter 1:
The Soulmate Myth

Your vision will become clear only when you look into your heart. Who looks outside, dreams. Who looks inside, awakens.

—Carl Jung

The word *soulmate* conjures up images of walking hand in hand along a secluded beach at sunset. Yes, I'm well aware that's the image shown on the cover of this book. It's there because that's exactly the type of image you first think of when you hear the word *soulmate*.

This romanticized notion of a soulmate as The One is continually reinforced in the media and in advertising for dating Websites. It's done more harm to modern relationships than just about any other concept I can think of. It sets people up with heightened expectations within their romantic relationships. No human being, not even The (mythical) One could maintain such impossibly high standards over the long term, through the ebbs and flows of years or decades.

This popular concept of soulmates often includes an added burden: the idea that we each have only one person (a single romantic soulmate) with whom we could be ecstatically happy, learning and growing together through life on physical, emotional, intellectual, and spiritual levels.

So let's get this straight right from the beginning: The popular concept that a soulmate is your one perfect romantic partner is a myth.

There, I've said it.

You can breathe a sigh of relief now because you already have soulmates—lots of them. The working definition of soulmate, based on my research into the origins and meanings of the term across cultures and throughout history, is a very simple one: *A soulmate is someone with whom you have a connection, a shared interest, an affinity.*

You Complete Me

The revered ancient Greek philosopher Aristotle left quite a legacy of wisdom. But when he said, "Love is composed of a single soul inhabiting two bodies," he missed one critical point of human life on earth: *We are each here to develop our own individual souls.* If you seek out complementary souls (your missing half, sometimes called a "twin soul"), you'll learn and grow together. You'll have connections, shared interests, and affinities. Through that journey you'll become soulmates, valued friends, maybe even lovers, along the road of life. But each of you is whole and complete, all by yourself. You are evolving and changing, of course. But you are still whole, right now, with or without a partner.

If you focus not on your own innate wholeness, but instead on whom you may think of as your missing half, you program your Personal Resonance with the belief that you are less than a whole being. Unless you really understand, deep in your soul, the principle that you are whole and complete right now, you will continue to attract others who feel they need a romantic relationship to be complete. A loving romantic soulmate relationship is a byproduct, a bonus of being self-aware and continually evolving. So, it all starts with you.

The Universe is far too efficient to allow you just one chance at anything, including finding soulmates who can evolve into romantic lovers. So don't panic if you think you've missed opportunities that may have been The One. You have many more chances than just The One. That certainly widens the world of potential romantic soulmates. There are many Ones, which I call Heartmates. That's good news. You have many more opportunities to find a Heartmate than you may have previously thought. Relax. Instead of panicking, put your energy into your Personal Resonance.

You may also find it helpful to redefine what a Heartmate means. Although some people do end up in one long-term relationship with a single romantic soulmate within their lifetimes, most people meet several in a lifetime. They learn and grow through their relationships. Each one builds on the ones before. So rather than seeking out The One for *all time*, take care to appreciate The One for *now*. That person is a mirror in which to better see yourself as you grow and change. They'll grow and change, too, and you may find yourselves looking at a long-term commitment. But if not, you can still find something for which to be grateful, something you learned from that romance. Even if it was only a great new recipe, be grateful. It's that attitude of gratitude for all of life's adventures and experiences that attracts more of them and keeps life interesting. It's a beautiful vibe to have broadcasting via your Personal Resonance.

Your Personal Resonance is the outward expression of your soul development and your intentions, even if those intentions aren't yet entirely consciously understood. Your Personal Resonance is the vibe or essence of who you are at a soul level that other people tune in to. Your Personal Resonance or PR is that soul-level light that you shine, the one made famous in that memorable song, "This Little Light of Mine, I'm Gonna Let It Shine." In a nutshell, *that's* Personal Resonance: your shining light.

Just as you might use a dimmer switch or a timer to add more or less light to a room at different times, depending on circumstances you can vary the amount of "shine" or Personal Resonance you send out. Essentially, you can program your PR, which includes all the soul development experiences and lessons you've learned so far in life (either this life, or all your lives if you subscribe to the reincarnation model).

If you've ever deliberately tried to hide energetically when around others, by lowering your shine when you don't want to be bothered, you already understand a bit of what I mean about programming your Personal Resonance. For example, I tend to "go invisible" on planes and trains quite often so as not to invite conversations when I'd prefer to read. It works so well that more than once someone's tried to sit on top of me.

By understanding what you're broadcasting (energetically speaking) through your PR, you can choose which elements of your personal programming to change to get what you want. Which means, in my traveling example, that if someone does take a seat next to me on the train, that person is likely to be on the same wavelength or Resonance as I am: someone who'd prefer to be left alone to focus on a book, or who'll exit at the next stop.

Remember: The level of shine you send out starts with *you*. You are in charge of your Personal Resonance, your energetic PR. So you are also in charge of the process of attracting soulmates because it's your PR doing the attracting. Think of your Personal Resonance as a giant magnet with the power to unerringly pull toward you exactly what your soul is asking for, even if you aren't sure, just yet, what your soul wants, or even what you (as a human being) want. Being in touch with what's good for your soul, by accessing your Inner Wisdom as a sort of life coach, is a smart move. It's also why this book is subtitled *Follow Your Inner Wisdom to Lasting Love.*

Outer Soulmates

Soulmate affinities and connections can be divided into three main categories. Let's call these types Outer Soulmates. Each of these types is a sort of lesson plan for you on a soul development level. Outer Soulmates can be found within your family, within your workplace, among your circle of friends and acquaintances, in your community, and certainly among your romantic partners. The three broad categories of Outer Soulmates are Karmic Connections, Balance Partners, and Heartmates, or romantic soulmates.

Karmic Connections are unfinished business, **Balance Partners** are your support team, and **Heartmates** are your romantic soulmates. A soulmate entering your life can start at any one of these levels. As they grow and change, so does their status with you. Once you clear up the unfinished business with a Karmic Connection, for example, you may become Balance Partners. From there, you might find that romance blossoms and you've evolved into Heartmates through time. You may also find that it's best to clear up the unfinished business and move on to other lessons-on-legs—

other soulmate relationships. And someone who once was a Heartmate can end up a challenge, a Karmic Connection. If you've got a troublesome ex out there, you know what that's all about.

When you feel a particularly strong attraction to someone immediately upon meeting him or her, seeing a picture, or hearing his or her voice or name for the first time, you are most likely dealing with a Karmic Connection. This is also true when you have an immediate, intense dislike of someone you've just met. Your soul-level lesson plan attracts exactly those situations in which you can learn the most through clearing up unfinished business. That strong initial reaction is often a clue that you'd be wise to tread carefully: This is karmic.

Life is never static. That's both the greatest blessing and the greatest frustration for most people. But the entire point of life on earth is soul-level learning through the human experience. But you can make the learning process easier on yourself and reduce your frustration levels. An attitude that broadcasts "I'm willing to learn, but please make my lessons as comfortable as possible" is not only wise, it's practical. This approach clearly states that you understand the point of the adventure—learning—but also puts forth your desire for the most efficient, pain-free method. Pain is, of course, part of life, but why take on more physical, emotional, or spiritual pain than you need to as part of the learning process?

You may not have much sense of control over the lesson plan you and your Inner Wisdom created before you arrived here on earth—the *what* and the *why*—but you have immense control over the *how* and the *with whom* aspects. Any learning journey has its challenging moments, as well as its joyful ones. And most of those challenges, and those joys, involve our soulmates, people who have an energetic affinity with us.

You can choose easier lessons; gentler approaches or harsher ones. Many people appear to enjoy suffering as they learn, or perhaps they don't realize there's another option, such as asking how to get to the paved road from this overgrown dirt path. You can also request revisions to the lesson plan. New soulmates to learn with and from. Remember: The goal is *soul-level learning*. The ways in which the lessons come, and from whom they come, are pretty much your choice.

This is wonderful news because much of the time a Karmic Connection relationship is not a joyful journey. It's unfinished business, after all. Tying up these loose ends often feels as if you've been down this road before (and you probably have). It's thrashing your way through the forest to create a path instead of walking along a smoothly paved road, only to find you're right back where you started. You've just wandered in a big circle. It's frustrating, it's inefficient, and it uses up a lot of energy. And it can rob your life of a great deal of potential joy.

Human Desire Versus Soul-Level Need

Sometimes what we *want* on a human level and what we *need* on a soul level are quite different. I myself wish it weren't so sometimes, but that's just the way it is. Still, we each have a measure of influence. It's done through what I call *declaration*, the process of putting it out there. If you never declare your desire for an easier way to learn a particular lesson, how can the Universe ever conspire to bring it to you? We're taught that, if we ask, we shall receive. Yet, most people don't live as if they fully understand that principle. They don't ask for an easier road. They muddle through. They struggle. They suffer. And it's needless.

By consulting your Inner Wisdom and talking it over, you can make your life much more fulfilling on many levels, but particularly with soulmates. Through the process of declaration, you can learn to attract different (ideally, better) soulmates of all three types into your life. You can learn from them in more powerful and efficient ways, by deliberately requesting a less challenging soul-level lesson. Or by reprogramming your Personal Resonance. Why take on a challenging, negative Karmic Connection to learn an important soul-level lesson if that same lesson can be learned more gently through a Balance Partner soulmate, someone who supports and encourages you?

If you're willing to first transform yourself through listening to your Inner Wisdom, declaring your terms, and reprogramming your Personal Resonance, you'll soon find your life rich with people in sync with your vibe. People who get you. People who understand and appreciate your Personal Resonance and who help you learn in ways that are, for the most part, joyful.

Don't worry—releasing the soulmate myth and embracing a Universe in which spiritual efficiency supports your life choices is not as difficult as it sounds. But to make this process as efficient as possible, you'll first need to understand three important principles:

1. Working with your Inner Wisdom.

2. Using what I call Now Power.

3. Exercising your free will wisely.

Attracting new soulmates and improving relationships with the ones you now have in your life requires one important thing: a willing spirit. If you're ready and willing, let the adventure begin.

Chapter 2:
Your Inner Soulmate

If I could see you, Spirit, all of the time I would ask myself then how would I act or think or be. Let me begin to believe that you are in the front of my eyes and in the back of my mind, witnessing every thought, every word, every endeavor—for you are.

—*Diane Cirincione*

Your Inner Soulmate is that aspect of your Inner Wisdom focused on your personal relationships with people you encounter throughout your life. Your Inner Soulmate is a sort of on-call personal or spiritual coach for relationships, romantic and other. This coach's job is to lead you toward the most rewarding soulmate-connecting opportunities, whether those are with friends, family members, workplace colleagues, or lovers. And she (or he) is accessible 24/7. Throughout *Natural-Born Soulmates* I use both terms, Inner Wisdom and Inner Soulmate, to represent your deepest Knowing, that part of you that's connected to the Source.

But just having a coach doesn't mean you'll immediately catch on to the process of intentionally changing your Personal Resonance. As the saying goes, "You can lead a horse to water, but you can't make him drink." In a similar way, your Inner Soulmate can bring you opportunities to experience soulmate relationships with others. It's up to you you decipher the signs, to recognize those opportunities, and to decide how best to complete the lesson to be accomplished between you and a soulmate.

Our lives are created through our decisions in reaction to the opportunities and challenges placed before us. Remember: It's the learning that your soul is calling you toward, not necessarily a specific or particular way in which the learning should happen. Are there some situations in which only one lesson plan, a relationship with one particular person, will be most effective? Certainly. But those are, thankfully, rare (and usually found within your immediate family, which provides many opportunities over a period of years to transform the situation). You've probably heard someone say, "You can pick your friends but you can't pick your relatives." Well, once you're here on earth, that's true. But your Inner Wisdom knows why you chose the particular life circumstances into which you were born, why you're in this particular learning lab: your family.

Accessing the Lesson Plan

Remember those three categories of Outer Soulmates? Karmic Connections, Balance Partners, and Heartmates, also known as romantic soulmates? Think of them as the Who element within your soulmate lesson: the type of soulmate are you learning this lesson from. Now, let's add to that the What of your soulmate connections: the overall theme of your interaction. Knowledge is power. The ability to identify the basic issues you are brought together to deal with what I call the Five Big Lessons, will help you to comfortably take on just about any challenge in the soulmate relationship department.

The Five Big Lessons are Passion, Purpose, Potential, Pacing, and Problem-Solving, which I'll discuss in more detail in future chapters. For now, keep in mind that every soulmate you encounter will have one (or more) of these Five Lessons woven into the tapestry of your relationship with him or her. By paying attention to the who and the what, you can give yourself a peek at the soul-level lesson plan. If you ask. And more importantly, if you listen for the answer.

Sometimes people feel that ignorance is bliss so they don't ask their Inner Wisdom, their personal angels, and other spiritual support team members, for help. Maybe they're too tired or too afraid to ask how they might change their life circumstances. Others simply never put the wise counsel of their Inner Soulmate into action. Instead they wait until someone else makes changes. That means they're left reacting to the choices of others. Their lives become designed by default, by the choices of others.

Do you want life on the terms others set for you? If you're reading this book, the answer is probably no. That action, alone, has begun the transformation of your Personal Resonance. Congratulations—you're already changing your life.

Turn Up the Volume

Perhaps you've heard the saying that the voice of your soul speaks in whispers. It's true. The information sent via Inner Wisdom often comes in soft and subtle ways, through symbols, repeated signs or references, synchronicities, or meaningful coincidences. Sometimes it feels that you're on a scavenger hunt, a process of piecing together a string of clues. Many people expect a strong baritone calling to them, similar to the voice of God in popular movies. They expect to hear that voice, that Inner Wisdom, with their ears, not with their hearts and minds.

Because what they receive doesn't match what they expected, often they dismiss those signs pointing toward the paved road. They never find the easier path toward to soul-level learning, because they aren't receiving *Big Signs*. They are seeing easily overlooked two-line classified ads, not illuminated billboards flashing "Thataway." By expecting Big Signs, they miss the helpful information their Inner Soulmate presents to them, bit by bit.

That's an easy issue to fix, as I've learned—the hard way, of course. Years ago I began to ask my Inner Wisdom to "make it unmistakable." Believe me, it works. I rarely miss a sign now, and to make learning soul-level lessons even more interesting, the signs I receive often come in highly amusing ways.

Not too long ago, I saw the very unusual name (both first and last) of a potential project partner scroll by in the credits of a late-night television program in a hotel in which I was staying. I'd been wondering about that very project only days before. Could it be I'd just received a Big Sign? To add a twist of humor, the program was broadcast on the Discovery Channel. That's what I mean by unmistakable. I agree more every day with a friend who calls the Universe "Chuckles" because she, as I have, has developed a bond with her Inner Soulmate based in large part on humor and joyfulness.

Another example of Big Signs involves a client who often received powerful signs from her Inner Wisdom via her dreams. Initially these were metaphors and symbols that she needed to interpret, so she kept a dream journal. Soon after I taught her to request that her Inner Wisdom "make it unmistakable," she dreamt the exact title of a book she'd never heard of, as well as the author's uncommon surname. Her first stop the next day? The bookstore. Naturally the book to which she was guided, which was nearly out of print and hard to acquire, as it was published long before, answered her questions about what direction to pursue in her life. She's a very precise person, and she got exactly that precision in return—just by asking her Inner Soulmate to make it unmistakable.

Many people receive similar signs via their Inner Soulmate, though perhaps not as strongly at first. They simply don't follow through on the insights about relationships that their Inner Wisdom is regularly dropping into their consciousness. They decide that it's crazy or illogical to follow such signs. So the signs become even more prevalent. Often the signs develop a negative element or more challenges because they were ignored. An example is a health problem that gives subtle signs of imbalance for a long time before turning into a disease. By heightening your awareness to the soft signs, you'll soon see those gentle clues are everywhere, as if they're blossoms dropping from cherry trees in spring.

You may resist guidance from your Inner Soulmate because you worry what others will think if you change your life in the direction toward which your soul is calling you. Maybe you worry about security if you change careers, or feel it's best to keep the family "intact" until the children are grown. These are all reasons that make practical sense, but they also focus on the material level, not the spiritual or soul level.

Resisting change for the comfort of others, or from fear, means that you really don't trust you Inner Wisdom. That's actually the same as saying you don't trust yourself either because you and your Inner Wisdom work together (or could if you learned to collaborate). You also may not realize the incredible power of your free will to choose another way, to transform your life.

Free will is the greatest gift you'll ever receive as a human being. It's the coin of your personal realm to spend as you wish. You can use your free will to resist the promptings of your soul's desire to grow. The tradeoff of using your free will to resist signs from your Inner Wisdom is often a negative change, or several changes in your life.

The event that turned my life upside down, and got me moving in the direction of my soul's promptings, was being rear-ended while stopped for an ambulance. It took a second rear-end collision, five months later, before I really began to change directions in my life. I was a slow learner back then, but thankfully, I pay closer attention now (four years of chronic neck pain was an unforgettable teacher).

Even so, I sometimes manage to ignore obvious, unmistakable Big Signs about my own path. For example, it took me several years after receiving an offer of free office space in a prime part of Manhattan before I based my consulting and teaching there. My reasons? I already had an office and I didn't want to commute into the city. Practical reasons, yes. Big enough reasons to resist my Inner Wisdom? No.

Free will allows you to move against, ignore, or not even tune into your Inner Wisdom. As I have you've probably done that many times. As you consider when you were guided and moved against that message, keep a record of the events and the consequences of your decision. You may be surprised at the patterns and themes that emerge. Just as mine is, your Inner Wisdom is nothing if not persistent. Eventually, I ended up in New York City, where I'm meant to be, at least for now.

The ability to hear the still, small voice of your Inner Wisdom becomes more reliable the more you consciously attune to it. You must practice listening, and be patient with yourself. As with any other relationship, the one with your Inner Wisdom requires time to develop greater intimacy and bonding, but turning your attention to the signs along the pathway of your life is a good way to begin.

What Does Your Gut Say?

Get out your journal or other note-taking device. Think about an important relationship you're currently in. Trust your instincts. Note your impressions regarding with which Who (Karmic Connection, Balance Partner, or Heartmate) and which What (Big Lesson) you're dealing in the relationship. Track associations that come to mind as you think about your personal history, your present circumstances, and what you feel is the ideal outcome of that relationship. Pay attention to your dreams over the next several days, too. Jot down what you recall. It's best to keep a recorder or notepad by your bed. Record the details as you remember them if you awaken during the night, or before you get out of bed in the morning.

Many people struggle to recall their dreams. If you don't remember anything from your dream state, work from your feelings as you awaken from the night's rest. Assess whether you're feeling anxious, sad, happy, gleeful, irritated, or resolved. Tune in to your emotional barometer every morning. If you still don't feel you're receiving information after using this technique for at least a week, don't worry too much about it. Just stick with the discipline of daily attention to signs and dreams.

Meditation or quiet reflection will also help you learn to better notice and interpret signs, those clues sent regularly from your Inner Wisdom. Even if it's just for 10 minutes a day, do what you can to get into that quiet zone where your mental chatter (such as mental list-making) is shut off, leaving room for your Inner Wisdom's voice to be heard. Everyone's busy, but here are a few ways you can blend meditation into your life without feeling that you're giving up something else that's important to you.

o While showering in the morning, or while relaxing in a bath, as the water flows over you repeat a focusing phrase, a mantra or affirmation. "I am calm, serene, and at peace" is one to try. Keep the language in the present tense; stay in the Now.

o While doing simple daily tasks such as washing dishes or folding laundry, or tending to pets or plants, create as quiet an environment as possible. If you like to listen to relaxing music, use a player and earphones to keep the sounds primarily "in your head." If you prefer a greater degree of quiet, use some foam earplugs to reduce the noise level. Then as you work, simply watch your hands move. Pay close attention to each gentle movement, to what you're accomplishing. When you find your mind wandering, which it will, bring your focus back by simply observing the movements of your hands.

o While waiting at appointments, or while sitting on airplanes, buses, or trains, instead of checking your voicemail or texting someone, use that time to close your eyes and focus on your breathing. Sit still, with your feet flat on the floor and hands on your lap. Follow your breath in and out, in and out. Keep your breathing even and steady, so that your in-breaths and your out-breaths use the same amount of time. You may find counting helps. If you don't have a focusing phrase or mantra, just mentally repeat something such as, "I breathe in peace" and "I breathe out stress." Keeping the words closely aligned to the event they're observing and attending to (in this case, breathing) helps many people who say they can't meditate. If you're one of those folks, keep your meditation activities simple, concrete, and easy to blend into your day, initially.

After you've finished your meditation, be sure to jot down anything that strikes you as you practice these simple, blend-into-your-day forms of meditation. Even the places your mind wanders are worth noting if they're consistent. Later you can determine if this place you wander to is a fear-based anxiety, or a sign of your Inner Wisdom at work. Your Inner Wisdom is never about fear, so if you're anxious or worried, that's you. Not sure? Just write it down and reflect on it later. Over time you're likely to notice trends and patterns.

The process of connecting with your Inner Wisdom is very similar to learning a new language. It takes time, focus, and especially practice. Trust in your own ability to connect with your Inner Wisdom, practice by making time in your busy life to allow your Inner

Wisdom to be heard, and you'll be surprised at what you learn about yourself—and by how much you've been guided all along, even if you weren't aware of that guidance process.

Now that you know how to become aware of your Inner Wisdom, just think how much more spiritually efficient you'll be, and how much more quickly you'll attract soulmates into your life who'll take delight in you, and add joy to your life.

Don't forget to ask your Inner Wisdom to "make it unmistakable." You don't want to miss an opportunity for a true soulmate relationship, do you?

Chapter 3:
Now Power and Your Past

Look to this day,
For it is life, the very life of life.
In its brief course lie all the verities and realities of your existence;
the bliss of growth, the glory of action, the splendor of beauty.
For yesterday is but a dream
And tomorrow is only a vision,
But today well lived makes
every yesterday a dream of happiness
and every tomorrow a vision of hope.
Look well, therefore to this day,
such is the salutation of the dawn.

—Kalidasa, 1200 BC

Where a connection between you and a soulmate originally emanates isn't that important, because it's changed since then anyway. Although you may enjoy musing about what past lives you and your soulmate may have shared, you're here, in the moment Now together. That's the only playing field you ever have in which to work things out: the moment Now.

All the connections between you and your soulmate, even those past lives, are simply forms of energy and vibration manifested in different ways. Any past unfinished business or loving bonds you two share, will, in the same way that a software program is, be automatically updated to the current version of your interactions. Now is the place you have the power to transform your relationship to its greatest potential.

Because the only place in which you have to work things out is Now, how you deal with your relationships Now (how you play the game) is what really matters. This is what I call your **Now Power**, and it's the most effective energy you have, particularly when you add your clear intention and free will to it.

You can use your Now Power effectively in your existing soulmate relationships to heal (not necessarily end or cure, but improve) troublesome relationships. You can use your Now Power to attract new soulmates to help you learn more soul-level lessons as you move along the soulmate path of spiritual development. What you do with your Now Power is entirely your free-will decision. The reason it's so powerful is that Now Power affects the past *and* the future. What you do Now resonates far beyond what you might imagine is possible.

Without sounding too similar to the author of a science-fiction novel or delving into spiritual interpretations of quantum physics and consciousness, I assure you that when you make a change in the moment using your Now Power, you also change both your past and all potential futures. That's a lot to take in: *Using your Now Power changes both your past and all potential futures.* Yes, that includes relationships with soulmates of all types: Karmic Connections, Balance Partners, and Heartmates.

This may sound confusing, but try to stay with me. Reread this section if you need to. It's important to understand the concept of Now Power fully because it's the key to transforming your soulmate relationships.

To make grasping this concept a bit easier, write down the phrase, *Only Now Has Power,* and place it where you can easily see it. Turn it into your computer screensaver. Keep it in mind as a meditation when you're exercising. Tuck it into your wallet. Mull it over until you get that "A-ha!" response, when it all falls into place and it makes total, natural sense. It'll happen. If it's confusing for the moment, just repeat to yourself, *Only Now Has Power.*

Now (sorry, I couldn't resist), what happened to you moment by moment in your past is still there, obviously. And although it has a vibration, an energy, it's not "alive" in the same way that the moment Now is. Those moment-by-moment adventures that comprise your life have been transformed into life experiences. Those life experiences have been integrated into the giant database of your soul's development. Essentially that database (sometimes called the Akashic record) contains details of all the things you've done, all the lessons you've learned, and all the soulmates you've encountered from the time you first existed. Certainly that database of knowledge is useful to draw upon as you think about what to do Now. But it's not "real" anymore. Your past is not vibrant and energized in the way that this moment, Now, is.

The Complacency Trap

Energy is dynamic: It flows. Every moment the energy between you and your soulmates of all types shifts. Making each moment count, making each successive Now powerful through conscious awareness, is difficult. But it's a critical element in building and maintaining the best soulmate relationships.

Too often, people get stuck in what I call the complacency trap. They allow their relationships to become static, to stand still. Their lives just sort of drift along. Their relationships with soulmates (including Heartmates) just...are. They are nothing exciting, but nothing awful either; not exactly boring, but not dynamic and flowing, either.

The complacency trap begins with a lack of attention to Now in relationships. People often feel that things will continue in the same vein indefinitely. They feel that promises made three or 11 or 27 years ago still stand, that there's no need to change or update things. "If it ain't broke, don't fix it" is the thinking behind this.

But if you never update your computer software, its operating system is at risk. Your computer may not be broken—yet—but it will develop problems if you don't tend to it. Your relationships also require updates and ongoing attention to keep them in the best condition.

So, if you're spending your Now Power energizing that "dead zone"—the static past rather than the dynamic Now—by thinking over your history together, you're putting your soulmate connections at risk. Your relationships with soulmates, romantic Heartmates included, lose that joyful, engaging energy that attracted you to each other in the first place. Through time, that loss of energy builds up to the point where you may lose your relationship entirely. It just tires out and fades. You must learn to bring things into the present moment, the Now. That keeps your relationships vibrant.

If you've ever been in a relationship with someone you felt was a romantic soulmate, someone you could never imagine life without, that ended, you may have fallen into the complacency trap. Maybe you felt that the present would always be like the past. Maybe you began to take the relationship for granted, based on promises made in the past or on your long history together. Perhaps you used your Now Power to energize something besides the romantic soulmate connection. Maybe you put it toward your children if you have them, or your education, creative pursuits, or career.

Whatever choice you made, you energized it moment by moment with your Now Power. Whatever your reasons—and they may well have been good ones—you made free-will choices about that relationship. Your soulmate made choices, too, in reaction to *your* decisions and choices. What you have Now is your joint creation. Only by realizing that you always had the free will to choose differently, by accepting full responsibility for the choices—good and bad—that you made can you begin to heal your relationship.

After you've assessed your decisions and their consequences, you can shift your Personal Resonance. Begin by bringing to mind your past experiences with a soulmate. Select experiences you'd like to be renewed and reenergized in the moment Now—romance or sexual passion with your Heartmate perhaps, playfulness with a sibling Balance Partner or a longtime friend, a sense of calm with a Karmic Connection.

Every day take a moment to think of three things about that soulmate that you treasure, love, or admire. Focus on soul-level qualities and personality traits, not physical attributes. Instead of saying, "I love his soft brown eyes," say something such as, "I love the shining brightness I see reflected at me when look into his eyes."

Keep the focus on Now by phrasing things in the present tense even if you're doing this exercise about a soulmate who's no longer involved in your life. Now is the only place you have power, including the power of gratitude and appreciation. And that is also your free-will choice. Even if a soulmate's free-will choices left you with significantly changed circumstances, you can choose to find gifts within those changed circumstances. What is good Now about your life? If you're breathing, you have something to be grateful for. Sometimes getting back to basics is the only way to find those hidden gifts.

Still, even in the most difficult situation, you can find lessons and things you can appreciate Now. If you divorced or ended a relationship with someone who cheated on you, for example, what's good about that? Well, for one, you're no longer with someone who doesn't place as high a value on fidelity as you do. That's a very good thing. You learned that perhaps you missed some signs of troubled waters with the relationship. Another very good thing: You're wiser Now. You've expanded that soul-level database and have information that will inform you as you make different free-will choices about romantic liaisons still to come.

But what if you're the one who cheated and you're feeling guilty about your choices? What's good about that Now? Well, you've learned that you are capable of having an affair, which probably seemed completely impossible to you at first. You learned you are human, and vulnerable, and that you seek love. Those are important soul-level lessons, too. You can decide to seek love in ways that cause less pain and heartache for yourself and others. Forgive yourself for being human and choose to operate from your Best Self from here on, starting Now.

It's actually pretty simple. It's *consistently* working from the moment Now that's the tough part. Think of adding pearls to a necklace: Moment by moment you'll create a longer strand once you learn to focus on Now. To get started, try this little exercise.

Breathe in slowly to a count of five and, as you slowly exhale, repeat aloud, "In the moment Now, I choose to be joy-full."

See? Instant transformation through the Now. You've already figured out how to shift your Personal Resonance to something that elevates your vibe, which in return attracts others with similarly elevated vibes. You've just created your first pearl.

Remember that those treasured pearls were created by irritation over time, starting with a tiny grain of sand in an oyster. Even frustrations can result in beauty. It's all in how you view things from this moment, Now.

Chapter 4:
Now Power and Your
Future

Love is the emblem of eternity;
it confounds all notions of time;
effaces all memory of beginning,
all fear of an end.

—Madame de Stael

As paradoxical as this may seem, when it comes to the future, only Now has power—the power of transformation, the power of choice. The past has no real power, unless you put your mental energy there, Now. Similarly, the future has no real power unless you put your mental energy there, Now. You can choose to place your focus on either point in the time stream, on history (past), or fantasy (future).

When you make a change in the moment Now you also shift all your possible futures, too. That may take a bit of thinking to fully comprehend. For example, you can decide right Now to purchase a ticket to Hawaii, find a job there, and stay. Suddenly your life is transformed by your choice. You may have dozens of (very good) reasons why such an option is impractical, but the bottom line is this: You can make transformations in your life, right Now.

You may feel you're "stuck" in your current life circumstances. Stuck with your current soulmates, those challenging Karmic Connections, those helpful and supportive Balance Partners, and even with your Heartmate. But you're not "stuck." You always have choice, the free will to choose differently in thought and action. *Always.* But every choice has consequences, risks, and rewards, which may be positive or negative. And, just to make things even more interesting, big decisions involve some of both.

Because only Now has power, the future is never fixed or destined. The future is flexible. The question to address is whether *you* are flexible. Is your fantasy of the future an escape from the current stress of now, or a plan to create a new, better life? The future changes with every decision, every free-will action you take. Certainly imagination plays a role. It's healthy to sometimes imagine yourself on a beach in the sun, relaxing, and getting away from it all—maybe even with a different Heartmate. But there's a difference between simply thinking about it, and planning a course of action.

Probability Theory

Think of the future as a story you're narrating, or a tapestry you're weaving. You may have a general plan for your creation, but nothing is so fixed it can't be changed. The future is fluid, dynamic, ever-shifting.

And that's excellent news when it comes to soulmates. It means anything is possible. Certainly there are parameters that define what is realistically *probable* in your life. You are probably not going to move to Hawaii tomorrow. Possible? Yes. Probable? No.

Besides having a good sense of what's probable and what's possible, having a grounded sense of what is realistic for you is important. If you are 5-foot 3-inches tall, the probability that you can become the next runway supermodel is very limited. But, if you aspire to the supermodel life, you can come closer to it through the choices you make. For example, you could put yourself in the arena. You could find a way to work in the world of fashion. Someone has to design the clothes, dress the models, manage their bookings, and select the best photos for the magazines and Websites. By widening your view, you increase your chances for happiness in your career. The same approach works in your soulmate relationships, too. Widen your view, open your heart, and be willing to try new things.

Besides a grounded and realistic view of yourself and a sense of adventure, for a life filled with enriching relationships with simpatico soulmates you must address the pile of consequences—the result of all those other free-will choices you've made thus far. Especially the ones that were reactions to the decisions of others. ("He cheated on me, so I went out and cheated, too.") Yes, this is the tough stuff.

Often the most challenging choices you will face are those in reaction to the not-very-enlightened or not-very-nice or not-very-compassionate actions of others. That's where you're likely to run into difficulties. Holding on to hurts and heartaches is also a choice, however. Ask yourself: *Does replaying that action-reaction cycle with someone I love get me anywhere that advances my life, Now?* Probably not. It only serves to dissipate your Now Power. Maybe it even adds a few choice ingredients such as self righteousness and perceived moral superiority. You might get to be "right" in such circumstances, but wouldn't you rather be happy? Then choose happiness. Now.

If you find yourself unable to release those old hurts, to integrate the lessons buried in them, and to move your focus to the moment Now, seek appropriate support. Find a credentialed psychotherapist with whom you feel at ease, and work out the knots in the tapestry of your life. Be patient. Listen to your Inner Wisdom about who can best assist you as you untangle the threads of the past. Many people find they search through two or three (or more) therapists before finding a good match or being fully ready for the inner work involved. Don't settle for the first therapist on your insurance company's list if it's someone you don't feel you'll grow to trust, to be emotionally intimate with. Investigate your options and talk to several people before selecting the right person to assist you. Treat yourself well. Scrimping on your emotional well being isn't a bargain in the long run.

Actions, Thoughts, and Getting Unstuck

As you consider what you want in your soulmate relationships, remember that your actions, as well as your thoughts, make a huge difference. Thought precedes action. But if all you do is think—ponder the past and mull over the maybes—you'll stay stuck in your relationships, and in all other areas of your life.

If you're prone to what's been called "analysis paralysis" or overthinking, you're giving your Now Power away. Instead of dissipating your Now Power with resentments about the past or worries about the future, why not use it to create the life you want?

Ah, but how do you get what you want in life? How do you even *know* what you want? This is where your Inner Wisdom can assist. But you'll need to make a pathway for that guidance. First, address the pile of consequences (karma) in your life. Sort out that emotional clutter. Next, focus on developing clearly defined goals and dreams about your future, goals with steps that you can begin to put into action, Now—and not the escape-from-reality type, either. Develop goals that you can energize Now with your thoughts, and later with your actions.

Developing clarity is important because, if you're confused, your Personal Resonance will transmit (and attract) confusion; ambivalence, if you're uncertain; fear, if you're afraid. Don't worry if you can't sort out right away what you really want. Often, it takes time.

As though blossoms on a tree which eventually ripen into fruit, the process unfolds in a very natural way in its own time. To fertilize and strengthen this clarity-creating process, focus on steps you can take Now. Even small steps in the right direction are better than none at all. If you're concerned about the "right" direction, relax. No matter what direction you choose, you will learn. If you focus on learning opportunities, there's never a "wrong" choice. And if you access and apply that natural Inner Wisdom, you're much more likely to make spiritually efficient moves.

Diversion or Desire?

An important question is whether your fantasies about the future are diversions, or situations you could actually manifest. Even if you think you're dealing with an actual goal, double check. Get out your journal and begin assessing. Discern whether you're enjoying a lovely mental diversion, an escape fantasy about the future that relieves stress, or a soul-level, Inner-Wisdom-guided goal for your life.

A client of mine wants to open her own healing center. She claims this is her goal, because she's had this dream for more than eight years. She continues to imagine what it would be like to give up the life of a busy corporate executive and run her own healing sanctuary. But what is she doing Now, in terms of actions, to shift that stress-relieving fantasy into an in-the-moment-Now reality? Very little. Unless her thoughts are backed by actions, she will never realize this dream. You've probably heard the saying that a goal is simply dream with a plan attached. In some ways, that's true.

By putting her fantasy of a healing center on paper in the form of a business plan, or creating an image of how it will look, by giving it a name, by taking *action* Now, my client could begin to program it into her Personal Resonance. By broadcasting her intentions on a vibrational level, she would then attract exactly the resources she needs. If she did take action, even just put it all on paper, she'd move her dream of a healing sanctuary from the world of thought (future/fantasy) to the Power of Now (action).

You may have heard of the Law of Attraction. This is, essentially, what you unleash by working on your fantasies in ways that empower them to become realities. That transformation begins with taking action. The way I see it, Action *creates* Attraction.

Consider the word *attraction,* and what do you notice? Buried within it is the word traction. *actions* add grip, staying power, to your vision. Embedded within the word *traction* is the word *action*. actions create traction—staying power—which leads to the next level: attraction.

What actions are you taking Now to create the foundations on which to build that future you desire? What "traction actions" are you taking Now to add stickiness, traction, or grip to the future you want to build? Believe me: Whatever actions you are taking have traction somewhere. So be careful to make them actions that serve you well in your quest to attract a soulmate, even your Heartmate.

Revising the Script

Even though it may feel uncomfortable to think of the future as entirely comprised of fantasies, some more probable that others, it's actually a very freeing way to see your life. After all, a fantasy is a story in which the storyline can be rewritten. You can create anything you want. And if you're willing to back up that revised storyline with appropriate actions, you can begin taking steps to make it real, Now.

You can use your Now Power to explore and create new life experiences. To script new storylines with different soulmates and happier endings. Or you spend your valuable Now Power reliving the past ("I wish I'd married him when I had the chance") or worrying about the future ("I wonder if I'll ever find someone who loves me"). Regretting the past and worrying about the future both deplete that Now Power that you could invest elsewhere.

Your Inner Soulmate knows it's time to start a new storyline. To rewrite your life script. If it wasn't, you wouldn't be using your Now Power reading this book about how to transform your life and your relationships. But I'm so glad you are—I promise you transformation awaits.

It can even start right Now.

Chapter 5:
Free Will and Soulmates

The one thing you can't take away from me is the way I choose to respond to what you do to me. The last of one's freedoms is to choose one's attitude in any given circumstance.

—Viktor Frankl, Holocaust survivor and psychiatrist (1905–1997)

Understanding how best to use your free will is where the real learning begins when it comes to your soulmate relationships. Because you are the one who chooses, you are also the one—the only one—responsible for those choices, and their consequences.

Shying away from this accountability within their relationships is why many people "freeze" within their lives. They get stuck, particularly when it comes to working out their closest relationships with friends, family members, colleagues, and romantic partners. Underneath it all lies a fear of change.

People fear negative change, understandably. They often stay in difficult or even dangerous situations because they're known commodities. But they also fear positive change. They fear what would happen if they reached out for more rewarding relationships with soulmates, and actually attracted them. They fear the new circumstances that any change might bring, including success—and its accountabilities. When they think it over, at least for the moment the known universe wins over the unknown, even though the unknown might be a far better situation. Maybe you have said something along the lines of, "If I could just snap my fingers and the change would already have happened, I'd be okay."

Change is challenging, there's no question about that. Managing the process of change requires ongoing flexibility. Learning to stay calm and centered, moment by moment in the midst of dynamic change, is a lifelong journey. But keep in mind that no matter what you think, or think you want, change happens.

In addition to change in your own life being a constant, within every one of your soulmate relationships (Karmic Connections, Balance Partners, and Heartmates), change is a constant. Whether you initiate it, or others do, change is an ongoing reality of life. Change *is* life. Even when you make no decision in a relationship—figuring it's best to leave things as they are—you're actually making a decision: a decision to defer your decision! Eventually you'll have to face the consequences. Wouldn't you rather use your own decisions as the means by which to change your life? Be proactive, not reactive? If so, you may as well use your free will at its highest level, especially with clear intention and guidance from your Inner Wisdom. This is the level at which what's best for you is known and encouraged, relentlessly.

But He Started It

When others use their free will to make decisions that, in turn, affect your life (such as deciding that your relationship is over), you may (understandably) feel frustrated, betrayed, cheated. Address those feelings first. Grief, anger, and sadness are to be expected. These emotions need to be felt and released for you to have the greatest degree of clarity. Your Inner Wisdom communicates best when you are centered, calm, and clear. That's why meditation is one of the best ways to turn up the volume on that still, small voice. But to get to that place, you must allow your feelings their voice.

After expressing your feelings appropriately (which includes doing nothing that you would be dismayed having others know about you or seeing on YouTube), bring yourself back to the moment, to deal with **What Is**: that the decision has been made by the other person. Fair or unfair, right or wrong, change has happened. Lament all you like, but realize that grousing only uses Now Power you could put to other pursuits. Just as reprogramming your Personal Resonance so that you can rise above the situation, react from a higher level, and with grace. The best reaction is always the one that elevates you, your vibration, and your Personal Resonance.

That Law of Karma, of consequences, is unavoidable. So using your free will to operate from an elevated plane of awareness, from a more soul- and self-aware position, is simply spiritually efficient. Even if you have to clench your fists and grit your teeth at times as you strive to react from your Best Self, that empowered place that expresses you at your highest vibrational level, reach for that place. You don't need the karma you'll create, the consequences that will ensue, from letting yourself react to a soulmate's free will choice from a less evolved level. Aim high as you respond to others. In the end, it works better than any other choice you could make in dealing with soulmates. Even when it hurts in the moment, it heals in the long run.

Resonance Rules

Your Personal Resonance is created with every free-will action you take, every decision you make. It's a vibrant expression of the consequences of your free-will choices. Your Personal Resonance expresses the unique "you-ness" of you. It broadcasts information on a vibrational level about all that you've been through, all that you've decided, all that helped you become the person you are today.

When you're challenged by the free-will decisions your soulmates make that you disagree with, remember that your free will is the only aspect of the situation between you that you *can* control. So use your intention wisely as you assess the best way to react. Pay close attention to the resonance, the vibe, the intention behind *your* reactions. What do you want this reaction to resonate? Are you acting from anger? From "I-told-you-so" self-righteousness? From "I'll-get-even-with-you-somehow" revenge? Face yourself honestly. It's not easy. But remember that high road often begins from a low place. Be patient and compassionate with yourself. Don't judge either party in the interaction—your soulmate or you.

The most spiritually efficient method is to use your free will to react to soulmate interactions (Karmic Connections, Balance Partners, and Heartmates) from the highest possible Personal Resonance. I repeat: Face yourself honestly. Then use the power of your free will to reach for the highest possible place from which to react. You'll not only feel better showing your best self, you'll add some additional shine to your Personal Resonance.

Also pay attention to how the communication or situation feels to you when you're facing the disconnect between what you "know" and what you're told. With soulmates throughout your life, you've experienced countless occasions when your gut sense was that the words and the feelings weren't aligned. That there was a disconnect between the intention and the communication. That you weren't getting the whole story.

The next time you feel that disconnect in your communication with a soulmate, whether it's your spouse or a coworker or family member, ask your Inner Wisdom for assistance in understanding the situation. Meditate for a few moments so that you can better listen to that still, small voice. Jot down your impressions about the situation. Let it flow. Write down whatever comes to mind. Pay attention to colors, symbols, and associations to past events that come to mind. Don't concern yourself with making full sense of your impressions right now. Just let yourself feel the disconnect and interpret it from that feeling-based level.

Write, draw, sing—whatever helps you express your feelings best. Let your instincts, your Inner Wisdom, your inner teacher called Intuition, guide you as you assess any challenging soulmate interaction. Often that deeply instinctual level, the place where fight-or-flight responses emanate when people are in physical danger, also has insightful clues about emotional and spiritual danger.

How many people do you know who just had a "feeling" that something was wrong with a family member's health despite test results that seemed just fine? Or that their child was lying about something despite protestations to the contrary? Or that their partner was having an affair and wouldn't admit it even when directly questioned?

These are all examples of Inner Wisdom and Knowing bumping up against the free will of others who choose to overlook, misinterpret, misrepresent, or lie about a situation or their true feelings.

You've been through similar situations, I'm sure. Times when others' free-will choices to ignore their Inner Wisdom—which always wants the truth to be presented with integrity and compassion—left you with some important free will choices of your own to make. Particularly how to react.

Do you match your soulmate at their level, or strive for a higher-level response? Do you raise the bar? You know by now that the spiritually efficient choice is to rise above the negativity. To shine more light on things. To actively transform the vibration, the resonance between you by using your free will wisely. At times it may feel like cold comfort, but your free will decision to come from a higher level in your response leaves a permanent elevation in the other person's energy field, too.

No, it's not always easy to take that high road, to be graceful in face of hurt and betrayal. But do you really want to deal with this same soul-level lesson, again and again? In this life, or a future one? With this person, or another soulmate who just picks up the script and continues in the role of villain? Use your free will to better yourself whenever you can, because others benefit, too. With such a powerful, spiritually efficient intention, you always win. Always.

And in the bargain, you create a bright, shining Personal Resonance that will attract a better quality of soulmates of all types. Including Heartmates, the ones that usually bring you both the greatest joys and the greatest challenges when it comes to being your Best Self.

But don't you want someone's loving Best Self in return? Then put it out there. Pay it forward. Resonate *your* personal best. To paraphrase the Buddha, be the change you wish to see in your life.

Chapter 6:
Surrender Your Agenda

We either make ourselves miserable or we make ourselves strong. The amount of work is the same.

—Carlos Castañeda

To attract the most beneficial soulmate relationships, you must let go of any attachments to a particular outcome, to surrender your agenda. Agendas are limitations, and in the soulmate search, you want the largest number of possibilities. Fewer agendas translate into more options. And when it comes to soulmates, particularly Heartmates, more is better. You learn the most, grow the most, and evolve the most on emotional and spiritual levels when you have more interactions with living lessons—your soulmates.

Agendas arise from our human, not our spiritual, natures. So when you focus on a specific outcome, when you hold an attachment or an agenda, your human self not your spiritual self or your Best Self is the magnet. Remember that whatever level you're resonating from will attract on that same level.

For the best soulmate connections, you must resonate from the level of your soul's Knowing, your Inner Wisdom, not the level of your human desires. If you think of this concept in terms of the chakra system, the goal is to operate from those higher centers of consciousness and energy to attract others who do the same.

Clearing your attachments is difficult because your agendas are often hidden ones. Developing an ongoing sense of nonattachment requires a consistent discipline, a persistent focus. But the payoff is what I call "bigger-better-more" experiences. Remember: Limitless living is the result of removing attachments and blocks—and agendas are blocks. Big ones. Boulders.

Agendas and attachments block your Inner Wisdom, your Inner Knowing from bringing you messages and promptings that, if acknowledged, will lead you to the love you seek, the joy you long for, the abundance you hope to embrace, the passion for life and for love that you once had. You'll find this with soulmates of all types, and especially a Heartmate.

Surrendering your agenda doesn't mean you can't dream of a soulmate relationship. Actually you need the concept of a soulmate relationship clearly in mind so that your unique personal vibration transmits, energetically speaking, that readiness. You need the concept, but not specifics, about a soulmate relationship. For truly powerful results, surrender any ideas you have of who your soulmate is, where that person may be, and exactly how, when, or why that person enters your life. And particularly what he or she looks like, does for a living, or earns.

Free yourself of all those limiting attachments, that human-level desire. Your attachments stand in the way of the best possible outcome from your soulmate search. Erase those limiting beliefs, those agendas. Become a blank slate. Next, focus on the *quality* of the experience you want to have with a soulmate as you move along the soulmate path. Make this as real as you can and spend time each day musing about life with the ideal soulmate relationship. Focus on how it *feels*, not on what that person looks like or any other details. Use that mental blank slate to store pictures, concepts, key words, and other elements of the experience you want to have with a soulmate or Heartmate.

Manifest the Best

Finding time to meditate and envision and manifest a trans formed life is always a challenge for busy people. I'm busy, too. But I've learned to delegate tasks to my Inner Wisdom to manage. That's what our spiritual guidance is there for: to assist us. And because I can use all the help I can muster, I put that Inner Soulmate to work as often as I can.

As you know, I'm passionate about being spiritually efficient in this process. I believe that if you really have a solid sense of your own power, you only need to intend something once for the Universe to hear you. If you need to say it twice, you're admitting you fear it may not happen.

Repetition is for *you*. The Universe doesn't need to be told twice. In the manifestation process, repetition is for *you*. It helps you learn. It helps you remember. It helps you focus. I repeat (no pun intended): Repetition is for *you*.

So when you use your intention to bring about certain situations, be sure to come from a place of confidence and trust, not of fear or anxiety. Surrender any agendas or ideas of specific outcomes you are holding in mind. Give your Inner Wisdom free rein to bring you the greatest possible learning experiences.

I often say, "Bring me the highest and best experience possible with this soulmate, and bring it in a joyful way" or, "I'm ready for bigger-better-more experiences: Surprise me with some new soulmates" when I delegate to my Inner Wisdom. Why not? As Carlos Castañeda said, "We either make ourselves miserable or we make ourselves strong. The amount of work is the same." I'd rather be strong and joyful, taking delight in the soulmates I have and the new ones I'll meet as I journey through this life. Wouldn't you?

As your personal spiritual coach for relationships, your Inner Soulmate is far wiser than you about these matters. A therapist friend sometimes puts it in more psychological terms, "Your unconscious is smarter than you are." But whatever you call it, trust it. Let your Inner Wisdom help steer the right soulmates in your direction for the person whom you are at this time in your life. What have you got to lose? Only your fears.

Tracking the Elusive Agenda

Surrendering your agenda means letting go of below-the-surface beliefs that are holding you back. But first you've got to track those agendas down. One example of an agenda, a limiting belief that's disguised in an often-heard statement is, "All the good ones are taken." Your Personal Resonance is largely based on your beliefs, so be careful to assess your beliefs and values, and to reprogram them from a positive perspective. (This block is discussed fully in Chapter 16).

Beliefs are the program code you write into your Personal Resonance. They establish the "vibe" you broadcast, and also what you attract. The belief that "all the good ones are taken" will resonate, and you'll attract people and situations that reinforce that existing belief. You'll become what a friend used to call a "loser magnet." She joked about the so-called losers she met. But even in jest, she reinforced her belief that she'd never find a "good one."

Maybe she liked the ego boost of being "right" and being able to say, "See, I told you, all the good ones *are* taken," to her friends. But I always felt she'd happily have traded being right for being in love. Her free-will choice to believe that she attracted only so-called losers kept her on a perpetual search for a true Heartmate. Her early death from cancer was even sadder to me because she never realized that she could have changed her outcomes by letting go of her agendas. She could have had so much more joy in her life.

It's as easy as writing some new personal code. After all, that particular notion isn't true anyway: Aren't you a "good one" in search of soulmates? Reprogram. Try something along the lines of "I am a vibrant person who attracts wonderful, available romantic soulmates." Update the broadcast you've been sending out. Begin the statements with "I" and keep them in the Now by using the present tense.

Use your journal to jot down your responses to the following statements, designed to help you get at some of your hidden beliefs about relationships. Write as much as you feel you need to. Later you can go back to notice what patterns emerge.

In romantic relationships, men (women) are _____.

Men (women) can't be trusted in romantic relationships because
_____.

Men (women) I date always _____.

Being hurt in romantic relationships with men (women) has changed me from a _____ person to a _____ person. (example: from hopeful to fearful, from relaxed to reckless).

Let whatever emotions come up arise to the surface of your consciousness. Take note of them. Feeling is freeing, so don't hold back. After a break at least a few hours, go back and see what patterns you discover in your responses. Look for a theme you can describe in a few words. That's one of your hidden agendas, now ready for you to surrender it. Repeat this exercise a few times within the next week. You may also want to substitute the word *friendship* or *the workplace* for the phrase *romantic relationship* to see what hidden agendas you are harboring in those corners of your Personal Resonance.

Although surrendering erroneous and mistaken beliefs may seem to be a rather passive mental activity, it's actually an active choice you make. It's your free will in action. Efficiently apply that free will by delegating your Inner Soulmate to direct you toward the highest and best experiences with all the soulmates in your life.

Over time, surrendering to the "highest and best" and allowing your Inner Wisdom to help will be become an ingrained habit; think of it as a recurring computer program that runs on its own and doesn't need much maintenance. Learning to surrender is a process; give yourself time. Be patient. But know this: It works.

Habits Die Hard

As you work on developing a deeper level of self trust, you'll have to you let go of (surrender) many ingrained habits. Grousing about the things you cannot change, such as the conditions of the river, for example.

You may have to let go of (surrender) your habit of seeing someone's potential, rather than the here-and-now reality of who they are. (See Chapter 13 for a more thorough discussion.) Who they are is shown through how they behave, not what they say. A loving person does not use violence. A kind person doesn't hurl insults. A person who values family spends time with family.

Living in the Now is much harder than living in the fantasy of "if only he/she would stop (or start) doing (name the desired behavior), he/she would be the best partner I could have." Deal with What Is, not what you wish for.

When you begin to face What Is, you may have to let go of the power of your history with someone you've been involved with for a long time. You may need to move on to new relationships. You may have to surrender some traditions and create new ones. You may have to risk the judgment, anger, or disapproval of others whom you care about. And you will definitely need to surrender your preconceived notions (your agendas) about what the perfect romantic soulmate looks like or does for a living.

Reprogramming Negatives Into Positives

Surrendering existing beliefs and agendas so you can reprogram them for greater spiritual efficiency also requires you to see the positive elements hidden within what appear to be negative situations. As an example, you could call increasing gasoline prices a negative situation, if you only consider the surface layer.

But chances are that, now, if you look at the situation more deeply, you'll find you actually enjoy some of the changes you've made in response to a change that was beyond your control. And yet, you can see the benefits in these I-never-would-have-thought-to-do-it-before changes in your life.

Am I thrilled that the price of gasoline is significantly higher in recent years? Of course not. But I also know my limits, and influencing oil futures and gasoline prices lies outside them. Yes, you could call this a let's-make-lemonade or don't-sweat-the-small-stuff strategy, but it works.

More importantly, surrendering yourself by releasing specific agendas, while also holding a broader vision of a soulmate relationship, is within the reach of your Personal Resonance, your free will, your intention.

This strategy of surrender-with-awareness works because it deals with the boat (that's you). You may have to flow with the river, the one made up of all the things you can't control—the free-will choices of your soulmates and Heartmates, essentially. But you can exercise significant influence on your journey along the river by deliberately shifting your vibes. By learning how to best steer your boat. By working with your Personal Resonance. By consulting your Inner Wisdom.

If it's challenging at first, ask yourself how well fighting the current, refusing to surrender to life's flow, has worked so far. Once you understand how to surrender the details, while holding a vision of your dream, you will find all your soulmate and Heartmate relationships change for the better.

All because you surrendered to your Inner Wisdom!

Chapter 7:
The Three Types of
Soulmates

If you would be loved, love and be lovable.

—*Benjamin Franklin*

Your soulmates help you learn more about who you are. You can't avoid lessons. They're what life is all about. But you can influence what living, breathing lessons in the form of soulmates you attract.

When you place your focus on attracting soulmate relationships, you magnetize them. Suddenly, soulmates of three main varieties—Karmic Connection, Balance Partner, and Heartmate (romantic soulmate)—seem to find you. They bring you opportunities to learn about your Personal Resonance, about the gift and responsibility of free will, and, most of all, about love in all its forms. It's done through those living, breathing lessons: your soulmates. Soulmate relationships aren't an easy ride down the river at all times, but adventuresome, absolutely. And isn't adventure why you're here?

As you read through the following descriptions (and the next three chapters, which examine these three types of soulmates in greater detail), you may find that certain people in your life—family, friends, and lovers, in particular—seem to fit into more than one category of soulmate. That's not uncommon.

Your former spouse may be a Karmic Connection who evolved first into a Balance Partner and later into a Heartmate who challenged you on many levels. Through the marriage it's possible your spouse moved back to the Karmic Connection level, repeating old behaviors that you'd thought had been resolved. By that point, you'd grown beyond a willingness to "go Karmic" again.

When you choose to hold a higher vibration, refusing to lower yourself to the other person's level, often long-standing relationships end. Other times, people stay in them, acting as chameleons which change their colors to suit the surroundings. That may work for a time, but when your true soul essence (what your Inner Wisdom is prompting you to recall and act on) awakens, you'll find it much more difficult to act in that chameleon-like fashion. You can't hide by matching your vibration to your surroundings any more. You've grown beyond the relationship.

The question to ask yourself when you end a relationship with a soulmate is: *What have I learned on a soul level?* This requires you to be well past the point of anger and to be more centered emotionally. When you lose anger, you gain insight. That's a pretty good tradeoff. Of course getting to that level of Inner Wisdom, of Knowing, of deep insight, is most effective when you're detached from any particular outcome, when you're not still "stuck" in the "stuff."

If the mention of your ex's name makes you want to scream, this isn't the time for insight. Be angry, if that serves you. But does it? Wouldn't releasing your anger with your ex free up your energy for some other purpose? And as some wise wag said, "Smile. It makes people wonder what you're up to." Learn to see the humor in the situation, even to laugh at yourself. It always lightens your vibration to be joyful.

Multitasking With Soulmates

Why do you often end up with one person who brings you Big Challenges to learn from—such as an ex who's a Karmic Connection, a Heartmate, and a Balance Partner, too? It's all about spiritual efficiency. It's rather like multitasking. Often the most spiritually efficient plan is for the same person to bring you different soul-level lessons you need. Just as an elementary school teacher might cover several subjects rather than just one, a certain soulmate may bring you many different lessons in various ways in one life experience.

Paying attention to the nature of your interactions with others will help you get the most out of your soulmate relationships with the least emotional and spiritual pain. You may wish to take notes in your journal about memories that arise as you read through these short descriptions of the three types of soulmates, especially about very influential people whom you've encountered in life.

The following are short takes on the three basic types of soulmates. Chapter 8 looks more closely at the Karmic Connection; Chapter 9 takes on the Balance Partner; and Chapter 10 delves into the Heartmate. Keep your journal handy: You're sure to find many messages from your Inner Wisdom bubbling up as you read and react to the next three chapters. Feel free to jump ahead if you're drawn to learn more about one of the three main types of soulmates. It's your journey, so take it in whatever direction you feel called to. Just pay attention to the process as you go.

The Karmic Connection, which I also called the "blast-from-the-past soulmate," is the most common type. Generally, these relationships are major involvements in your life, but that's not always true. Karmic Connection relationships are based on unfinished business, things that were left unresolved between you in a previous existence (or experience) together. Whether positive or negative, Karmic Connection relationships are the consequences of past choices in past lives, manifest before you now as living, breathing lessons. Or, they may result from actions you took in this life.

Lessons sound as though they're work. But there are many ways to learn lessons, some easier than others. You may prefer the joyful, fun, creative approach to learning. If you'd rather have the stern, stodgy, harsh approach, go for it. If you've never thought about how you'd like to learn, take some time now to mull it over. Jot down your insights in your journal. Write down some affirmations: statements of your choice in the matter, phrased in the present moment Now. You might try something such as, "My life is rich with joyful interactions with others from which I learn all I need to on a soul level" to begin. Allow your Inner Wisdom to guide you to the words that best suit your situation at this time.

Sometimes, the unfinished business or karmic debt that one person owes the other takes decades to resolve, perhaps even lifetimes together. Other times, the karmic debt is so small that you might not even recognize until later (if at all) that you've connected and worked out your business together. By developing a consciousness about soulmates, as you're doing by reading this book, you'll soon find yourself able to identify Karmic Connections easily, even those that represent brief involvements and quick clearing of karmic consequences of prior interactions.

The Balance Partner is someone who shares with you an important goal or common ground. Balance Partners are treasures in your life. These are the valued friends who can be truly happy when you receive a promotion that could also have been theirs. These are the much-loved siblings you resonate with, and support as you together live with an alcoholic parent or another form of difficult home environment. These are the coworkers and colleagues in whose presence your creativity and skill level seems to be exponentially enhanced. Together, you draw strength from each other, support each other, and help each other through challenging times. You're teammates in life.

Balance Partners often are at the center of your most enjoyable, stable, and long-term relationships, whether with friends and family, with creative or business partners, or in romantic involvements. But no matter in which area of your life you encounter a Balance Partner, the connection always has a very synergistic quality. What you accomplish together seems far beyond what you might expect from only two individuals.

Many times Balance Partner relationships evolve from initially challenging Karmic Connections. If you've worked with someone for five years, for example, developing a powerful friendship over time, you're dealing with a Karmic-Connection-becomes-Balance-Partner situation.

Balance Partners often help you find your place or purpose in life. A Balance Partner could be a parent, child, spouse, or lover, or any other influential person whom you feel has led to you toward a more fulfilling life experience. Very often your parents, whether birth parents or adoptive parents, serve as Balance Partners, as do other influential adults in your childhood.

Many times Balance Partner connections are brief. A teacher who notices and encourages a particular talent may serve as a Balance Partner, guiding you toward the best expression of your gifts and talents. A minister, rabbi, or other spiritual adviser who helps you understand the spiritual circumstances of your life could also be a Balance Partner in your life, if only briefly. A boss you had early in your life who instills a passion for a particular type of work is another example of a Balance Partner. A therapist or a counselor who helps you in the process of healing, or a medical professional who helps you through a lengthy illness also may serve as a Balance Partner for a specific period of weeks, months, or years. A "rebound" relationship after a serious breakup can be a form of Balance Partner soulmate connection, particularly if you found that you rebuilt your trust in others, or rediscovered your sexual passion. Lovers, even those you don't keep for long, help you transform and evolve. Don't lament that the relationships "didn't go anywhere." Celebrate what you learned in this kind of Balance Partner/Heartmate interaction.

Remember the book *How Stella Got Her Groove Back* by Terry McMillan (Viking, 1996)? Stella is, well, let's say transformed through her interactions with a much younger man. As with the case of the fictional Stella (and the real-life Stellas you know), even brief romances have the power to help you learn and grow. It's not about the sex, either. It's about what you learn about yourself through the sex. Did you learn to become more open and free? Did you learn to allow yourself a more profound level of pleasure? Even a brief fling has a lesson in it, if you look for it.

Not all soulmate connections are lifelong interactions, whether Karmic, Balance Partner, or Heartmate. Length of time spent together is not a way to measure the success of any relationship, no matter how brief. Instead of berating yourself for making a "mistake," think about what you learned. There are no mistakes from the perspective of your soul. Only lessons learned. Only more data for the database.

Many times Balance Partners are meant to inspire you. No debts are owed to them or due to you. This type of soulmate relationship enters your life to encourage you to better your own best efforts, to go beyond what you think is possible. Just as the hard surface of a stone can be used to sharpen a knife, Balance Partners sharpen you. They push you beyond what you think you can accomplish. Though it's often a challenge, it's also a breakthrough. Challenges can be enjoyable, particularly when you've managed the challenge and you're reflecting on what you accomplished. The memories of the difficulties you overcame fade as the glow of accomplishment brightens.

Balance Partners are often those people you find particularly irritating, whether they are family members, friends, teachers, colleagues, or lovers. Through the challenges of a Balance Partner, you make important, if difficult, breakthroughs in self awareness. The end result is always positive. Just as you had to learn to play team sports in school with people you may not have liked very much, your Balance Partners aren't always folks you would pick for the team if you were the coach. But Balance Partners always help you evolve into a better player in the game of life, and if you're going to play in this game called life, why not play it well?

The Heartmate is a romantic soulmate. This is the type most people associate with the word soulmate. As discussed in Chapter 1, the Soulmate Myth is the idea that there is only one person with whom you could be ecstatically happy.

Generally, this romanticized notion is accompanied by a fairly long list of attributes that are based in the material world: hair color, height, weight, income, educational level, and so on. This list is often completely unrelated to a person's level of *soul* development. As discussed in future chapters, attachments to particular attributes in a Heartmate actually limit the possibilities of attracting such a person.

If you really want a romantic soulmate, a true Heartmate, a partner to share your life, you must look to the *soul*. Seek beyond the obvious. Be adventurous: Has playing it safe worked so far? Let yourself be surprised by the intriguing possibilities your Inner Wisdom will present—if you let it. Broadening your perspective and looking deeper will enhance your success.

A Heartmate relationship is the type of connection in which Personal Resonance, being in sync in terms of wavelength or vibration on physical, emotional, spiritual, and soul levels, forms the core of the connection. The sense of being completely accepted and understood, of feeling safe and at ease in that person's presence (and still connected when you're not together), is a hallmark of a Heartmate or romantic soulmate relationship. Heartmate relationships grown out of Balance Partner relationships are always more stable than those based on Karmic Connections. So, if you're hoping to attract a romantic soulmate, pay attention. If you have challenges from the beginning, you may be dealing with a Karmic Connection. Those challenging connections can evolve into higher levels of soulmate interaction, but it's much more work. The spiritually efficient path encourages you to focus on balance in yourself and others as the foundation for any relationship.

Keep in mind Heartmates don't always stay in your life. Not every romance is forever. They can teach you in many ways, and some of those may seem "negative" to you, as pain is part of the process. But perhaps a short affair that reminds you that life is too precious to waste on anything but joy is exactly the lesson you needed at the time. When it comes to food, for example, what's good for you nutritionally doesn't always taste the best (Brussels sprouts and spinach, anyone?). Your soul has spiritual needs in the same way your body has nutritional needs. Adjust. That's simply the way it works.

If you think about it, a blissful life of ongoing lovey-dovey interactions, writing poetry and songs for each other, walking hand in hand into the sunset, wouldn't be all that blissful as a steady diet. Too much of a good thing—chocolate or cheesecake, say—will make you sick on a physical level. The same is true on a soul level: A steady diet of bliss becomes rather boring and is unhealthy. You need what I call "compare-and-contrast" moments to remind you to be grateful. Without the challenges you wouldn't appreciate the bliss nearly as much. Balanced nutrition, balanced interactions with soulmates; ups and downs, sweet and bitter—all experiences, tastes, and flavors have their place in that database of your soul development.

Even when you have a sense that a particular Heartmate inter-action may be short-lived, I encourage you to explore the possibili-ties. After all, being someone's lover allows you to learn a great deal about yourself, as well as about the other person. Whether that learning is positive or negative or the relationship lasts only months not years is a separate issue. The point is to ask, *What did I learn about myself?*

Learn to be grateful for those soul-level lessons, whatever they are. Doesn't it feel good to know that, say, you've got the lesson on infidelity handled? Phew. You don't have to do *that* one again. You can now move on to, say, tantric yoga to learn the joys of physical and sexual expression when it touches the divine. Or you can con-tinue to send out a Personal Resonance Pattern that continues to in-vite that same lesson, over and over, with new Heartmates. You choose.

Remember that any soulmate relationship includes ups and downs, challenges and rewards. Karmic Connections, Balance Part-ners, and Heartmates are all part of the river of life. You wouldn't want the river's current to be smooth and gentle all the time, would you? Where's the adventure in that? It's the rough rides over the rapids that you'll learn the most from at the soul level. Soulmates challenge you to use skills you didn't even know you had.

Whether Karmic Connection, Balance Partner, or Heartmate, soulmates bring out even more shine from that divine soul essence, your Personal Resonance, that unique *you* vibe. A true soulmate helps you express your essence, your unique and special self.

Your Best Self.

Chapter 8:
Karmic Connections

The kind of seed sown
will produce that kind of fruit.
Those who do good will reap good results.
Those who do evil will reap evil results.
If you carefully plant a good seed,
You will joyfully gather good fruit.

—*The Buddha*

Karmic Connections, those "blast-from-the-past" soulmates, are the most common type. Generally, these relationships are major involvements in your life, but that's not always true. Karmic Connection relationships are most often based on issues that were left unresolved between you in a previous existence together, but sometimes you're helping the other person learn an important lesson, playing a critical role in his or her personal development. When resolved, those challenging Karmic Connections have the potential to become supportive and loving Balance Partners in your life. Maybe even Heartmates.

Karmic Connection soulmates are those folks who show up in your life whom you seem destined or fated to encounter. Whether it's within your family, among your friends, or in your romantic life, Karmic Connections are the people with whom you experience the greatest struggles. They're unfinished business that you need to deal with on a soul level, lessons that you've not yet completely mastered. They're the ones who seem to know how to "push your buttons." Often Karmic Connections are the "final exam" of a particular soul lesson, before the dynamic shifts to a Balance Partner relationship. Sometimes you're taking the exam (learning how to bring balance); other times you're giving the exam (serving as an example of how to bring balance). Either way, there's a test of some sort involved, and often, it's your patience that's being tested.

Once Upon a Time

Even if you can't recall how things began with a Karmic Connection, that challenging soulmate probably is someone you've known far longer and better than this lifetime alone would explain. The intensity between you could only result from lots of shared lifetimes and experiences. Troublesome Karmic Connections can be found in any area of your life: the workplace, the family, among friends, or in your romantic life. Some people attract Karmic Connection soulmates in several areas of life, but generally they tend to cluster in one area. That's because your Inner Soulmate encourages you before you're even born to limit your Karmic Connections to one arena, a single playing field, such as work, family, or romantic love relationships. Taking on too many lessons would work against your success.

You may know people who seem to shine at work but face repeated challenges in romance, or who never seem to sort out their careers but have long-standing, loving bonds with family members, friends, and spouses. It's spiritually efficient to cluster your soul-level lessons in this way.

Keep in mind that karma as I use the term in *Natural-Born Soulmates* is simply the consequence of an action. Karma isn't payback, punishment, vengeance, or reward. Repeat: Karma is not payback, punishment, vengeance, or reward.

It's just a record of outcomes, a tally of consequences. It is a sort of spiritual bookkeeping record. Karma just deals with What Is—the tally, right here and now. Because all you ever have is the moment Now, Karma is always a current accounting. And because choices in the moment Now affect both your past and your future, when you get the hang of dealing with Karmic Connections, you can clear up a lot of unfinished business very quickly. That's where listening to your Inner Wisdom comes in.

Compassion in Action

Whether it's physical or spiritual life, consequences cannot be avoided. But conscious awareness helps you consider the possible consequences before you act. That's wisdom in action. If you remember that karma is simply the reflection of your past actions and reactions to the choices that others made, you may begin to see family members and others who are very close to you in a different light. Do this by listening closely to your Inner Soulmate, whose job is to help you even out and balance your life so that you reap as much joy and learning as possible.

Immediate family members are almost always Karmic Connections. The family is the hub of the karma wheel. Sometimes that karma, the consequences of your previous interactions flows easily between you, in a nice even balance, creating a Balance Partner soulmate connection. (See Chapter 9 for more on Balance Partners.) If it doesn't, you can use your free will and Now Power to uplift or shift their resonance, their vibe, by uplifting yours first, by electing to serve as a Balance Partner. It's not always an easy choice, but the best thing about your Personal Resonance is that, as does the light from a shining star, it extends light years beyond what you may think is possible. You don't need to be face to face to employ your Personal Resonance effectively with someone. Your intention to shift the vibration is enough to begin the process.

Taking weeks, months, or even years away from interactions with certain family members (often parents or caregivers if you've had a challenging childhood and adolescence involving emotional, physical, or sexual abuse, for example) may be the best decision for you as you seek to heal and release your unfinished business. You can always go back to the relationship later if or when you feel that's appropriate.

Consult your Inner Wisdom to help determine the most spiritually efficient course of action. Sometimes, it's getting away—and staying way—that you are to learn. That even bonds of family ties don't give permission for people to abuse, hurt, or neglect others. If you were living near a toxic dump, you'd do all you could to move away. Sometimes, people are the "toxic dumps" in your life with which you must deal. In such cases, the soul-level lesson is a simple one: Move away. Save yourself from the toxic energy. Stay strong. Create a different life in a safe place.

You still have power to change the situation no matter how toxic. But you don't have to do it face to face. You can program your Personal Resonance with loving compassion, and send it through your focused intention, or prayer, to those who've hurt you. But, for your sake, do it from a safe distance, whether emotional or physical or both.

If you choose to leave a toxic situation unaddressed, don't berate or blame yourself for a lack of action. That highly efficient Law of Karma will ensure you'll have an opportunity in a future life (or while in the spiritual realms when you leave this life) to set things back in balance. By that time the person involved may have grown enough spiritually that resolving the issues between you is much simpler. By choosing to be the Balance Partner in the dynamic, even if that means to step away for a time, to send loving thoughts but stand away from one-to-one interactions, you elevate your Personal Resonance. And by your intention, theirs.

Working Out the Karma

Maybe you know people who've been in a long marriage that doesn't seem happy to outsiders, but that, to the parties involved, feels right to stay in. Perhaps you yourself have stuck it out in a particular relationship, whether in a job you no longer enjoyed, in a friendship you'd outgrown but kept anyway, or in a marriage or other long term partnership that was just so-so.

Get out your journal. Take time to assess your motivations in such cases. Take a good hard look at the tradeoffs you made, and the karmic consequences that resulted from your choices. Were you involved to focus on the other person's needs, perhaps tending to someone with a chronic illness? If so, your intention and motivations had a high purpose: service to another.

Through such service you're sowing what the Buddha would call "a good seed" and you can expect good fruit at harvest time. But maybe tending to someone else's illness allowed you an excuse to stay hidden from the world. You served someone else's needs, yes, but you also cheated yourself. Your own needs went unmet. It's all about balance. You matter, too. You are a high priority, too—or should be.

Be careful of falling into what I call the caretaking trap. Many people, particularly women and natural nurturers, give so much of themselves away on behalf of others that they find themselves depleted, resonating fatigue, and seething with low-level resentment. With all the demands on their time, they're not overflowing with joy and gratitude from moment to moment. And what do they attract? Often it's tired, resentful partners, ex-partners, and kids—others who aren't overflowing with gratitude.

Being conscious of your attitude and bringing as much joy to the process moment by moment, using your Now Power, can transform others as well as yourself. So even when you're tending to mundane tasks, perhaps endless piles of laundry, with a touch of resentment, focus on what you can be grateful for in the moment. Start with the fact that you and your family have enough clothing, and the help of a washer and dryer. Gratitude attracts gratitude. As German mystic Meister Eckhart wrote, "If the only prayer you ever say is 'thank you' it will be enough." Before long others around you will say, "Thanks," without being reminded.

Quick Karma

Sometimes the unfinished business that needs to be released between you and someone else is so light, so easily and quickly resolved, that you might not even recognize you're involved in a karmic soulmate situation. Keep in mind the definition of soulmate is *someone with whom you have an affinity, a connection.* Based on that definition, you've run across many thousands, maybe even millions, of Karmic Connections through your adventures in soul development.

You're dealing with Karmic Connections on a regular basis, whether you're completely aware of them or not. So by presuming that everyone you meet is in some way a Karmic Connection, or someone who needs your support as a resonance-enhancing Balance Partner soulmate, you will make choices that help others as well as help you develop on a soul level. Doing so is a very wise choice: It's very spiritually efficient.

A situation in which a brief but powerful interaction has transformative power is offering what you learned by experience to someone else who could benefit from that information. If you have personal experience dealing with a misdiagnosed illness, for example, you might post your insights in a blog or forum. You may never even know that you've helped someone, but you could possibly lead others to make important health changes through such a simple act as extending yourself. Through sharing what you've learned along the Soulmate Path in your life thus far, you transform both yourself and others.

Karmic Consciousness

Some Karmic Connections are lifelong; others arrive for a single occasion, and others last for weeks, months, or years. By developing a consciousness about Karmic Connections, as you're doing by working your way through *Natural-Born Soulmates*, you'll soon be able to identify them easily, even those which are momentary involvements or very brief interludes. Those who are serious Karmic Connections, the ones that have big lessons for you, are easily identified by paying attention to your immediate, initial reaction.

The "power punch" reaction: If you experience an immediate reaction to someone you meet, either positively ("I feel as if I've known him forever and we just met") or negatively ("there's just something about her I don't like, but I can't quite put my finger on it"), pay attention. Energetically speaking, that instinctual reaction is a "power punch" and it's a major clue that you're dealing with a Karmic Connection soulmate.

When you experience the power punch, be careful, particularly if you're embarking on romantic or business-related interactions. You don't want to skate right past red flags about that person just because you feel comfortable right away. Stay in the moment. Take your time. Let these new-on-the-scene Karmic Connections reveal themselves slowly.

Don't compare a potentially Karmic soulmate you've just met to a wish list (read: agenda) that you keep or to another person you've known. Evaluate the situation. Wait to see if it's superficial charm, or that person's true inner soul that's attracting you. Some weeds start out resembling pretty flowers, after all. And be especially careful if you've ever jumped into a physical relationship quicker than, say, the amount of time you've spent on a shoe-shopping trip. Learn to savor the slower journey.

The "frozen moment" experience: Often when you on past relationships that you feel are Karmic Connections, you're forever after able to recall quite distinctly the very first time you laid eyes on that person, or first heard his or her voice. "Love at first sight" is actually a sort of energetic memory of that person that overshadows the moment you first meet in this existence. The frozen moment experience is particularly common with Karmic Connections who have been romantic involvements in past lives, or who could become Heartmates in this one.

If you can easily recall the moment when you first encountered certain people, they are probably Karmic Connections to you.

The more detail you can easily remember, including sounds, sights, and physical reactions, the stronger the karmic bond—and often, the bigger (and maybe more painful) the lesson you're to learn together. The more you can recall from a first impression, and especially if you can recall it in striking detail years or even decades later, the more likely you're dealing with a Karmic Soulmate. So even though you may enjoy those "pow" impressions from your Karmic Connection soulmates (including those referred to as "love at first sight" when it's a romantic soulmate), remember that unfinished soul-level business, unlearned lessons are the foundation of your connection. Once resolved, you may part—or you may grow into Balance Partners or Heartmates. Go slowly, pay attention, and, of course, ask your Inner Wisdom for support.

Even Karmic Connections with whom you have a very brief interaction can leave such distinct "frozen moments" as clues to the soul-level power of your encounter. I once met a nun in an airport. She was taking her first airplane trip in more than 30 years, on her way to visit her sister who was dying of cancer. At age 93, this frail nun needed a bit of help to make her way around the terminal.

As I extended my arm to her, that by-now-familiar "frozen moment" feeling signifying "pay attention to this one" came over me. In that instant, my Inner Wisdom informed me that this nun, whose name I never learned, was a karmic soulmate to me, although we spent fewer than 20 minutes together. When she handed me an inexpensive blue plastic rosary (she was a Catholic nun, after all) as we were about to board the plane, she told me that although I wasn't Catholic she knew I was a very spiritual person. I was suddenly near tears.

That strong reaction completely surprised me. Because of it, in that moment, I knew from that deep level of Knowing that we had cleared up whatever unfinished soul-level karmic business we needed to. I'm pretty sure it was something to do with past lives and a convent.

This is a good time to get out your journal and consider times in your life when you've had similar experiences, powerful encounters that shaped you, touched you, or taught you. Write down or record your thoughts and impressions about who the Karmic Connections in your life have been. You might find it helpful to break your list of Karmic Connections into three areas—family, work, and romance—and start with one area. Write down what you've learned from them, and also what you feel you taught to them. You are an important element of that dynamic. They learned from you, too. Far too often people forget to honor themselves for their contributions to their relationships. So include in your journal what you gave to those important Karmic Connections in your life.

From Karmic Connections to Balance Partners

After the unfinished business between you and someone else is resolved, you're dealing with a different sort of soulmate connection, what I call a Balance Partner. To help you grasp this concept, think of that familiar infinity sign, the Arabic number 8 turned to its side. On a soul-development level, this symbol represents the steady flow of energy between you and someone else. When both loops are equal in size, the flow continues indefinitely, forever. Infinitely. Neither loop is depleted of energy, or clogged up with too much. As you assess your life and your relationships, keep the goal of easy balance (as shown by the infinity symbol) in mind.

By working from that little "X" at the intersection of the two loops of the infinity symbol, that very balanced place (think of it as Now), you develop a Balance Partner consciousness. That beautiful balance becomes a feature of your Personal Resonance that attracts—you guessed it—other balanced people. And if you're planning on a long-term connection with someone, balance is always a good thing.

Chapter 9:
Balance Partner Soulmates

No one is useless in this world who lightens the burdens of another.

—*Charles Dickens*

As you seek to attract soulmates into your life, especially if you're seeking a romantic connection, a Heartmate, you'd probably prefer balance to chaos within your relationship. You'd probably prefer that easygoing, synergistic flow that's so well represented symbolically by the infinity symbol. Because you know by now that what you broadcast attracts on the equivalent vibrational level, you also know that it all starts with getting your own Personal Resonance in balance.

Balance Partner soulmates are gifts. They deserve your gratitude and appreciation. They're your teammates in the game of life, ready to rally you on. You do the same for them. Balance Partners are true friends. They are completely and utterly pleased for you when you accomplish something you'd set your sights on. Balance Partner soulmates are big enough in spirit to congratulate you—sincerely— when you receive a promotion that might have been theirs, or when you attract a romantic soulmate, a true Heartmate, before they do.

If you've found yourself in the role of Balance Partner to someone else, you know that a slight twinge of "I wish it had been me" is quite common. It's a natural human reaction. But if you're honest with yourself, you also know that as soon as that feeling passes, in many cases a beautiful, unselfish excitement for the other person emerges. That's your soul essence, your Best Self, shining through.

Keep that familiar (and unavoidable) Law of Resonance in mind. Realize that actions on a particular vibration (whether low or high) ha~e consequences on that same vibration (whether low or high). So why not aim high when you react to the events in the lives of others? You can't avoid the Law of Resonance, that river you're riding along, so you may as well work with the current, not against it. You'll get farther, faster that way. It's much more spiritually efficient.

Inspirational In-the-Moment Balance Partner Soulmates

Witnessing what's possible for others just shows what's possible for you. Sometimes people you don't even know serve as In-the-Moment Balance Partner soulmates for you. They inspire you. If they can get there, so can you. Here's an example:

Interviewer: "How did you end up on full scholarship at this prestigious university, given that you spent 12 years in 17 different foster homes, some of which were abusive?"

Successful Young Adult: "Well when I was 13, I saw a guy on TV, and I thought, 'Hey if he could get through that horrible childhood in foster care, and end up at the top of his class and go on to college, I could do it, too.' So next year when I'm done with my medical residency, I'll be working with underprivileged kids like I was. Maybe I'll be able to inspire somebody else."

Balance Partner soulmates such as these are treasures in our lives. They represent moments when our Inner Wisdom speaks to us through others. You may never know whom you've affected in a similar way. When you sit down with your journal to consider who had this kind of momentary-but-profound effect on your life, realize you've probably done the same for others just as many times as a Balance Partner to *them*. Don't get caught up in a need for feedback. Being in balance means you're unaffected by what others think, trusting in your own Inner Wisdom, your own soul's insights. Just let yourself be embraced by that soul-level resonance, of your own power to transform by example. Leave your human ego aside. And revel in the power of your Personal Resonance, the essence of your soul, the real you.

One day you'll get the whole story of your impact on this world by having been in it. That's the day you leave this world to return to the place where it all began, at the Source. But while you're here in human form, you may as well take as many opportunities as possible to transform this world for the better.

Perennials: They Just Keep Turning Up

Year after year, lifetime after lifetime, as though they're perennial plants in your garden certain soulmates return, and return, and return again. How can you identify those perennial soulmates, those Balance Partners, in your relationship garden? If you pay attention to the shared energy, the resonance between you, you'll realize you already know them.

Your Balance Partner soulmates are the ones with whom you have an instant "click" of understanding, with whom you feel at ease right off the bat. Their energy is comfortable, familiar. They're the old reliable plantings you can't imagine your garden without. They're in your life to support you, assist you and keep you laughing as you deal with the other soulmates in your life, particularly especially challenging Karmic Connections and Heartmates.

Often you have a sort of telepathic no-words-are-needed-to-communicate connection with your Balance Partners. You often find such steady, supportive soulmates in extended family relationships such as with grandparents, aunts and uncles, step-parents and in-laws. Best friends from childhood usually are Balance Partners. Very often first loves in adolescence and young adulthood are Balance Partners, often having had Heartmate connections in previous lifetimes. They come into our lives to remind us of the power of love, even when the different lessons this time require that the relationship be a short one.

This powerful connection is why so many people who lose a spouse to death or divorce seek out those first loves and find that rekindling that old flame is natural. Of course, many others discover those first loves were big lessons in the form of Karmic Connections, who may or may not have evolved to Balance Partner status by working on themselves and their Personal Resonance. If the situation is well balanced, if both parties have sorted out this lifetime's lessons, a reconnection to a first love can be one of life's greatest blessings. Timing is everything and, often, the best time is later, when you're both more spiritually evolved.

As you help Karmic Connections balance their lives by serving as a Balance Partner, a good example, extend yourself in the other direction, too: Allow Balance Partners to assist you, just as you assist others. You are as much a teacher as you are a student in life, and one of the rewards of helping others is receiving that help when you need it. The tough part is acknowledging your need for Balance Partners.

Your Inner Wisdom knows when you need Balanced Partners, and sends them your way, particularly when life is difficult. When you lose someone to death. When you face an illness. When you find changed life circumstances because of job loss, career change, or divorce. As you reflect on key events in your life you may discover you've had many more Balance Partners soulmates, those earth-based angels, than you ever realized before. (And yes, Balance Partner relationships often continue even after death, in the form of spirit guides, the term often used by psychic mediums to describe an after-death Balance Partner bond.)

This is a good time to jot down in your journal encounters with people, even brief ones, which helped you bring your life back into balance. Don't overlook short-term Heartmates who served the role of first-one-after-the-big-breakup, what you might otherwise consider a "rebound" relationship. They may have ended but they also helped you learn to rebuild your life. The ability to be gentle with yourself about such relationships, to see the learning found there, sets you on a good course for even better Heartmate relationships.

The Allure of the Familiar

Familiarity is alluring. Comfort is seductive. Just like the story of Rip van Winkle, years may pass while you're resting comfortably, staying well away from the soul-stretching, personal growth-enhancing relationship challenges of life. Such familiar circumstances, although comfortable, mean you're trading off some learning opportunities.

By limiting your world primarily to Balance Partners with whom you've already got a lovely back-and-forth flow of Personal Resonance, you miss opportunities to help and support others, as well as to add to that soul database.

It's appropriate and wise to take some "comfort breaks" among your familiar and supportive Balance Partners as you tend to your relationship garden. You do need to stop and smell the roses. But when the time feels right, get back to the business of attracting new life situations and Balance Partners soulmates to help you learn and grow. Invite your Inner Wisdom, that helpful Inner Soulmate, to guide you in that quest as you tend to the garden of your relationships.

The "Above It All" Trap

Be careful not to remove yourself from the learning opportunities found only here on earth, among your fellow human beings. For example, if you're someone who feels you're "above" workplace politics, too elevated as a person to delve into those lower vibrations, you may react negatively to the very idea of serving as a Balance Partner in that negative environment and stay as far away as possible.

But maybe the reason you're in such a negative working environment is because you're needed there, to show others how to elevate themselves. To learn how not to allow your higher vibration to be lowered. Your Personal Resonance is elevated, and others around it are elevated, too. You can learn to consistently hold that high vibe so that it has the greatest impact. You can learn to access your Inner Wisdom for support and shielding what I call the Process of Declaration, being of clarity. Declare yourself off limits for negativity on the level of Personal Resonance. You're the one writing the programming, remember. You are the one who, using your free will, declares what you will and will not accept on that level, and every other level, in your life.

Whether it's within a toxic family environment, a difficult marriage or a negative work environment, when you're faced with such situations, act from what I call your Best Self level, that high vibration you can achieve by allowing yourself to be a vehicle for that universal wisdom you access via your own Inner Wisdom. Shine that Personal Resonance as brightly as possible. Serve as an earth-based angel, as a Balance Partner. You can have an effect. You already do, so you may as well intend that it be big and bold and powerful. The bonus is that it's much more spiritually efficient, too.

Be the best example of a human-being-divine as possible through the intentional use of your Personal Resonance. By doing so, you become magnetic to those who can learn from you. Supporting others as a Balance Partner means you must be willing to connect on whatever level they come to you, and trust that your strong, clear, powerful Personal Resonance will affect theirs in positive ways.

Being a Balance Partner to others isn't necessarily easy. It means you may end up in some pretty negative environments or places of lower vibration. See them as what they are: places needing your shining light, your Personal Resonance. You can begin the process of transformation very easily, by reframing how you see a particular situation. That alone transforms things.

By being open to other interpretations, you expand and elevate the interaction between you and your Balance Partner soulmates who need your example. You reprogram your Personal Resonance. Then everybody wins, particularly you, because you've lifted things to a better-than-before, higher-than-it-had-been vibe. Others may choose to follow your example, and raise their vibes, too, continuing the process you set in motion. And soon enough, an energetic ripple effect, your Personal Resonance ripple effect, is spreading—changing the world. This is all because you learned to see the so-called negative in a different way: as a situation that needed rebalancing with your Personal Resonance in the mix.

Group Adventures: Soulmate Improv

You have Balance Partner soulmates who interact with you primarily one on one when it comes to providing support. But you also you interact Balance Partner soulmates in group adventures. It's what I call Soulmate Improv.

Think of yourself and your soulmates as improvisational actors who together create a play or a sketch, on the spot, in the moment

Now. You really don't know how it'll turn out from moment to moment. In these interactive improv experiences with your soulmates, your life can take huge turns in directions you never, ever expected. Your friend becomes your boss. Your husband becomes your ex-husband. Your friend becomes your ex-husband's latest lover. You get the idea: Any role can change at any time. All you ever know is what *you* are supposed to do. And you can change that, too. Which means that in the game of Soulmate Improv, there's no absolute or destined outcome you can count on. Just as in life.

Any Balance Partner in your soulmate improv troupe can shift the group Resonance, change the vibe in a big way, at any moment. The guy playing Hero suddenly wonders what it would be like to transform into Villain. So he tries it out. Now you, fellow soulmate improv troupe members, must make some choices in reaction to his decision to change his Personal Resonance from Good Guy Vibes to Villain Vibes. (If you've ever had a challenging breakup or a nasty divorce, you know what this particular improv sketch is all about.)

You have power, too. You can also change troupes in this Soulmate Improv and seek out different adventures if things stray too far. You might look at another Soulmate Improv group and think, "I bet I could learn a few things from that bunch; I've learned all I can here." So you move across the country, or out of the country, or change careers. It's yours to create through interactions with your fellow Soulmate Improv players: your Balance Partners.

Sharing the Spotlight

If you continually take on key roles in improv sketches you develop with your Balance Partner soulmates, the other improv players don't get the chance to stretch and grow their skills. And guess what? You also create a Personal Resonance that shouts "big ego" or "diva" or "control freak." And because that natural Law of Resonance never falters, you'll attract that very same vibe somewhere else in your life.

If you've ever known a very capable, high-achieving coworker who had no problem taking charge at work to phenomenal results and support, but whose home life seemed totally out of control, you've witnessed the Law of Resonance in action. It's as if this person didn't understand that his role as Boss among the Workplace Improv Soulmate Troupe was not welcomed in the Marriage and Family Improv Soulmate Troupe, which has a whole different sketch evolving. Flexibility is required.

Soulmate Improv, as a metaphor for life on earth, is a reminder of the power of your Personal Resonance. That being fully centered in the moment Now matters. That you are both teacher and student, director and actor at every moment. And that flexibility matters. No wonder you need Balance Partners for help and support!

Repeat or Delete

Discerning your soul-level lessons is assisted greatly by asking your Inner Wisdom for guidance, but it also requires you to reflect on your life, and tease out themes and patterns you may not see on the surface. You're the one writing the programming for your Personal Resonance. So you're the only one who can rewrite it. Do you want to repeat the same lesson, or learn it and delete it from the lesson plan so you can try something else?

Here's an example. If you've ever been part of a work-related project team or a difficult family, and found yourself thinking along the lines of, "If they'd only let me run things, we'd be in much better shape," you've probably discovered that you aren't the best collaborator. If learning to collaborate is one of your soul-level lessons this lifetime, your Inner Wisdom will bring you a series of Balance Partner soulmates in your life, with whom you can play a good game of Soulmate Improv until you figure out how to collaborate, how to serve as a Balance Partner for others, and how to receive insights and guidance from others.

A clue to the lessons you're supposed to work on with your Balance Partner soulmates is found in the repetitive experiences and themes. Learning to break out of those comfortable roles and try on something new, to play around, to improvise, takes more than one opportunity. Yes, often it feels as though it's neverending. Many times it's presented as a negative situation—a term I suggest you change to *learning experience.*

As you think about repetitive themes among your relationships over the years, whether with family, friends, or lovers, also think about how you can change up the role you're playing in this interactive improvisation called life on earth. Think about how you've served as a Balance Partner for others. Remember times when others have served as Balance Partners for you. Watch for repetitive themes. Use your journal to record your thoughts, feelings, frustrations, and hopes about how your life could be different.

Changing your life begins with you, with changing the role you're playing, with changing your Personal Resonance, by impovising something better. And you can do that anytime.

You can do that Now.

Chapter 10:
Heartmates

We love because it is the only true adventure.

—Nikki Giovanni

Ah, romance. Who doesn't enjoy the heady rush of flirtatious banter, of anticipating that first kiss, of being courted, of falling in love? Romance is definitely a feature of human life that makes its less-enjoyable aspects fade into oblivion, at least temporarily.

Among the best-selling categories of fiction books are romance novels. That's not surprising, given the abiding allure of the romantic soulmate, what I call a Heartmate. And yet, a "perfect" soulmate, a one-and-only love whom you're destined to meet and spend a lifetime with, simply doesn't exist. There is no "destiny": All that free will in action, all those choices of billions of humans on the planet take care of that. There is no "perfect" either: The dynamic flow of constant change means what's perfect one moment is changed in the next.

Though it may be difficult to let go of the fantasy of The One, by doing so you open your world up for much more love. When you can learn to live with appreciation for the ongoing adventures in life, with gratitude that options abound in all areas of your life, your life expands. And with it, your possibilities for finding a Heartmate, a romantic soulmate with whom you can evolve and grow, learn, and enjoy life and all it has to offer. You can attract love at the right time, for the right reasons. The soul-level reasons.

Those soul-level reasons, believe it or not, include sex. A true Heartmate relationship includes a good deal of sexual chemistry because that's one of the ways human beings lift themselves out of the mundane realities of human life (jobs, dishes, traffic).

If you don't immediately feel excited by the touch of a new possible Heartmate, you may have the foundation for a terrific Balance Partner. Without chemistry, it won't evolve into the kind of Heartmate bond you'd really like, one that resembles those romance novels. But the connection might surprise you if you start from that place of balance and fondness. You may find that the slow burn creates a lasting fire.

But aren't you supposed to meet certain people? Yes. Back to the Soulmate Improv troupe. Before you're born, certain situations are established regarding your life on earth. It's an outline, your rough life plan, sort of the bare bones of an improv sketch. You develop this plan with the help of your Inner Soulmate and other guides. You determine things such as into what particular family and in what particular place you'll be born.

Next, you develop a sort of set list of various improv sketches: "I'll start with Difficult Childhood, move into Accountant, then into Divorced Father of Two, and wrap up with Happy Traveler." It's a soul-level lesson plan detailing what you're here to work on with other soulmates: Karmic Connections, Balance Partners, and Heartmates. You're likely, *but not destined,* to encounter certain people as you work on those lessons.

Just as you have, they've decided to join this particular Soulmate Improv experience. But things can change: Remember free will? A few soulmate-actors might keep reappearing, or nearly appearing, so that you have the opportunity to meet and work in a sketch together. But sometimes the role has to be recast: One actor is unavailable, so a different one takes on the role of Heartmate for you.

Keep in mind that Heartmates also evolve here on earth. Karmic Connections can evolve from unfinished-business-to-sort-out into supportive Balance Partners, and from there into Heartmates. Even if you never connect with one of those soulmate-actors you and your

Inner Soulmate identified before you were born as good for a par-ticular role in your improv experience, *you still have many thousands of possibilities to find a Heartmate.*

This built-in redundancy, this failsafe system, this spiritual effi-ciency, means that getting through life without at least one roman-tic soulmate, one Heartmate connection, is just about impossible. Which means: you cannot get through life without love somewhere. Unless, of course, You decide to program your Personal Resonance with a lot of blocks to attracting a Heartmate. (To learn about the Five Big Blocks see chapters 12 through 16.)

Whether your evolving improv sketch weaves together in a cre-ative, cohesive way depends on the in-the-moment decisions you make as you play off the Resonances, the vibes of the other players in your improv troupe—aka your life. Your ability to listen to the other actors, and support and encourage them as they perform their roles, is critical to the success of your improv sketch.

When you meet someone whom you feel has the capacity to grow into a powerful Heartmate, pay attention. Treat this person as someone with whom you're doing an improv exercise. Listen closely to what that potential romantic soulmate is actually saying before you react and build on what they toss out. What you actually hear can be greatly influenced by what you want to hear. Pay attention to What Is.

If you've ever witnessed someone suddenly become much more interested in a potential introduction after learning the person earned a high wage or owned his own business, you can be fairly certain that heightened interest is not from a soul level. If she really wanted a Heartmate, a true soulmate connection, she'd ask about his likes and dislikes. His values and interests. Those are the connection points between soulmates, the things they can jointly resonate around. She'd be concerned about the man himself at a deeper level and not just what he does for a living or how much he earns.

Of course, if two people come together to create a successful busi-ness, as Balance Partners who later evolve into romantic soulmates, the resonance between them is based on their common interest in business. That's authentic. Unless the woman who shows sudden interest in earning potential also suddenly finds telecommunications or cement contracting or investment banking fascinating, she's probably not being authentic about the reason she's intrigued by this new man her friends want her to meet. She has a not-so-hidden agenda: to build financial security through someone else's efforts rather than her own.

That may be fine, as long as she's honest about it to both herself and the fellow her friends want her to meet. Maybe he wants someone around to pamper or take care of. Maybe he wants a relationship with a dependency dynamic rather than to engage soul-level-to-soul-level, equal to equal. Rarely do people own up to their agendas in the flush of new romance. But those who understand the Law of Consequences, also called karma, know that hidden agendas lead to occasions when others, in turn, hide their real motivations.

Honesty really is the best policy because, on a soul level, you can't hide. Your Personal Resonance tells the whole story even if you never speak a word. So, wise Heartmate-seekers learn to "read the vibes," to intuit and interpret the Personal Resonances of others. (See my book *Natural-Born Intuition* to learn about your intuitive style.)

Quality Versus Quantity

Be careful not to judge the success of the romantic encounters thus far in your life by the length of time you are together. After all, time is an illusion: There's only the present moment Now from your soul's perspective. The quality of the time you spend together matters more than the quantity of time you spend together. You probably know people who've stayed together for 10 or 20 years or more, but whom you'd never say have a successful romantic relationship on a soul-to-soul Heartmate level.

View potential romantic soulmates as improv partners, people with whom you can create a scenario in the moment, a scenario that can go in any direction. It may last a short-but-joy-filled period of time, in the same way that a hysterically funny bit which lasts only a few minutes but is remembered always. Or it may lead into an improvisational sketch that has "good bones," that forms the core of a longer play. A play that might last for years—maybe decades—featuring a script that's always being expanded and improved as the players evolve and deepen their characterizations.

Rewriting Your Romantic History

Most people don't take the time to fully assess what they've learned in life, and apply it to relationships in their lives, Now. But by doing so, you can turn your experiences with Heartmates into practical working wisdom. You can even rewrite your relationship history and through that process, transform your life. You can start right Now by writing what I call a Heartmate Review. If your relationship with a former lover were a movie, what would you write about it if you were a film critic? It's time to find out.

Get out your journal and write a few paragraphs about a romantic relationship you were involved in that's ended. Play the "movie" in your head. Make notes as you watch your inner movie. What's the overall tone? Is it a thriller, a comedy, a drama or something else? Next, write down five to 10 descriptive characteristics about the lead characters in the roles they're playing. Do this for both your former love and yourself. Assess your role in this movie of your life with that same sort of detached, careful observation you'd use as a film critic. Jot down the reactions you have to key plot points.

Now, rate the movie on a scale of one to five stars. How many stars do you give this drama, action film, romance, or comedy? Two? Four? Five? If you were the director (and actually you are), what would you change about the movie so that it has a better ending? Really allow yourself to feel deeply about the experience shown in your "movie." Imagine as real a rewritten script or follow-on sequel as you can. Make notes throughout this review and assessment process because through time, if you conduct this exercise with several different relationships, whether romantic or otherwise, you'll soon see the types of roles you choose to play. You'll also see what types of actors you cast within your movies.

An added bonus of this "movie review" assessment process is that it transforms your past as well as your future. Just as your future has many possibilities, none of which is fixed or destined, neither does your past remain fixed. That may sound confusing, but think about it: It's simply the other end of the spectrum, the continuum of time. The past operates exactly the same way as the future does. It's just at the other end of the spectrum, the continuum. Just as the future is malleable, so is the past. Nothing in your past is absolutely a certain way, just as nothing in your future is. Why? Because your view of the situation, even of a past event, can always change. This concept may be challenging at first, but it's true: Even your past can be changed. No, not the events. But your perspective.

You can use your Now Power and your free will to see a particular event in a new way at any moment that you decide to do so. Because of that powerful freedom of choice, nothing in your life—your past—is destined to remain fixed, to always be a certain way. Perspective matters. How you reframe things as you garner wisdom along the road of life matters. So, because you can change your view, nothing is absolutely fixed. Even a completed past event can "change"—because your viewpoint can change.

As an example, when you reframe a hurtful comment from a playground bully who impacted your self-esteem negatively ("you're stupid" or "you're ugly") to instead see it as the uninformed view of a child lashing out at another child, the sting dissipates. You might even develop a feeling of compassion for the bully who lashed out, as well as for the child in you who took that on, and carried the weight of it all these years.

You can release your past view, and literally change your past, transform it, right Now. Just by seeing events of your past differently perhaps with greater compassion. Perhaps with gratitude for lessons learned, perhaps through the eye of your Inner Wisdom. However you choose to see the events of your past, realize that you have great power in how you tell the story of your life, absolute free will about how you direct the movie of your life. Remember: You can always edit.

You can rewrite the script with any experience with your romantic soulmates of the past, or even the present. You can create a different ending, or leave room for a sequel. You can cross out scenes you don't like—leave them on the cutting room floor, as the saying goes. You can edit your film so that different aspects of the interactions between the characters are emphasized. You can change the motivations of the characters involved. Play with the script. Perhaps you want to cut the scene where you have a messy, public argument with your former Karmic Connection, and substitute instead the scene in which he stands next to you at the funeral of a much loved relative, offering you support as a loving Balance Partner at a time when you really needed it.

The viewer's feelings about any character in a film change as the director's viewpoint changes. What would happen if your cheating ex wasn't cast in your movie as a cad anymore, but instead as someone afraid to be hurt? The cheating ex becomes a man who grew up in a home divided by divorce. A man afraid to put all his focus, all his attention, on one woman who might leave, just as his mother did.

If that loving relationship with his wife ended, he might feel that his world would collapse, just as it did when he was 4. To avoid being vulnerable a second time to the emotional devastation he felt when the most beloved woman in his life suddenly was gone, he spread this risk of being hurt across more than one relationship. You can see the logic (albeit the logic of a child) in this scenario. He ended up of course with far more hurt, more lost love, and more messy consequences (and more karma to clear up) because of his affairs. And mostly because he'd never looked closely at the impact of his earlier experiences (feeling the loss of his mother when he was just a child).

Write new backstories or character histories for the people in the movie of your life, including you. Find other ways to explain their motivations. You may surprise yourself with your ability to find compassion blooming towards someone within what was once a hardened heart. This isn't exactly forgiveness, but an exercise in seeing things a different way. An exercise in using your power in the moment Now to rewrite your life on an energetic level. Remember: Your consciousness doesn't recognize anything but what's in your mind right this moment, Now. What you place there, what occupies your mind, how you think of your past and your future, affects them both Now. And if you choose to forgive after this exercise, you may find yourself experiencing emotional freedom in a way you never expected, or could even believe was possible.

Back in Balance in an Instant

Here comes the really mind-blowing part: You can settle unfinished business, with both past life and current life Karmic Connections, by reprogramming. By rewriting the script. By changing the "story" with which you're so familiar. You know, the one you tell when asked about your last relationship on a date: She lied, he had a drug problem, she was more interested in work than in me, he didn't ask me to marry him so I left, her kids hated me, he wanted to take a job transfer to another state that I said I would never move to.

Clearing up past "stuff" (aka baggage) is done through the focused use of your consciousness, by exercising your creative power in the moment Now. I really do mean creative: Your goal with this exercise is *to create a new past as well as a new future about that relationship right Now*. You can clear the karma in any relationship, even those long past, even those from previous lifetimes. You can also stop yourself from creating more consequences, except the type you want.

Whatever that familiar story is, change it. Try it as an exercise in your journal. Use your imagination. Soon you'll soon see that a change in perspective changes everything about your romantic soulmate involvements, and your other soulmate involvements as well. And hopefully by now you've come to understand that you can take the joyful journey, the smooth ride down the river, instead of the scary one over the rapids, but the rapids may teach you more: it's your choice.

By cleaning up unfinished business your Personal Resonance becomes more clear and powerful. You'll find that you naturally attract new opportunities with a higher level, a higher vibration, a better matched Resonance, soulmate to soulmate. But avoid developing attachments to specific outcomes or people. As you already know from Chapter 6, attachments limit your possibilities for soul-level growth.

A certain level of desire is fine. You need to have a passion, a vibrancy, a palpable excitement about having a romantic soulmate, a Heartmate, in order to attract one in the most spiritually efficient way. But, developing a passion for a particular physical look, profession, or any other characteristic grounded in the physical world is unwise. It limits you. Your Inner Wisdom, your own Knowing, is trying to teach you an important lesson: *to focus on the soul of a person not his or her outward presentation to the world.*

Just to reiterate: Desire is not attachment. Desire for love is one thing; attachment to love from a particular person in a particular way is entirely another. Desire is the *what*; attachment is your (limited) idea of exactly *how, when, where,* and *why.* Let your Inner Wisdom sort that out. Expand your horizons. Desire a state of being, nothing more. As in, I desire to love and be loved.

Discerning between desire and attachment isn't an easy process, particularly when it comes to Heartmates, and particularly in a world in which goals, plans, and outward appearances are held in higher esteem than inner being, soul-level values. Everyone, of course, has preferences—some people so strongly that they develop fetishes. That's definitely too strong an attachment to a particular attribute for living a balanced life. The goal is to be flexible, open to possibilities.

By learning to acknowledge desire, but also to sublimate your preferences and open yourself to other possibilities is a process. It will take time. If you've always had a thing for brown eyes, expand your horizons to include blue-, green-, and hazel-eyed people among your possible Heartmates. Would you want to risk missing out on a Heartmate bond over something such as eye color? Or height? Weight? Or ethnicity? Or hair color or personal style? This same line of reasoning applies to all the people out there who put "no bald men" or "must be 5 feet 8 inches or taller" or "must weigh 130 pounds or less" in their profiles at dating Websites. Desire without attachment. Put it out as, "I desire this or something even better for me at this point in my soul growth and development."

I've known women desperately seeking romantic soulmates (or so they said) who rejected men over their shoes or the style of shirt they wore on the first date. So, what if the guy is fashion-challenged? Is it his shirt or his soul you're interested in? Maybe the superficial attributes, the material (and I don't mean his shirt) that attracts (or repels) certain people. The superficial ones. What you attract is the result of what you've been resonating.

Be honest with yourself. Some people are perfectly happy trading happiness for financial security (think sugar daddy) or financial security for appearance (think trophy wife), for example. If that's the Personal Resonance you want to broadcast, that fleeting superficial aspects such as money (gone when you leave this world) and looks (which change with time) are your focus, go for it. But don't be surprised if you find yourself on a date with someone who rejects you because your hair isn't blonde enough, or long enough, or who feels you need to lose weight before they'd consider you datable. Personal Resonance attracts on the same vibrational level. Superficial attracts superficial. Soul attracts soul.

If you spend an hour or so with someone on a coffee date, and he says, "I'll call you," and you never hear from him again, it's not because he didn't like your soul. When did he have a chance to connect with you on that level? Getting to know a person at the soul level takes time. Months, not weeks or days. That's something that most people find difficult in this busy-busy-busy, now-now-now world we live in. No wonder they end up in messy situations from moving too fast. And that includes rejecting others too fast, as well as being rejected too fast.

Keep in mind that your Personal Resonance extends to your personal style and presentation. The care and attention you pay to your grooming, to the condition of your clothing, to your hairstyle and makeup, even to your teeth and your shoes, your home and your car, and especially your health, show the world whether you value yourself. Whether you care enough about yourself to invest that precious commodity (time) into your appearance and your surroundings. If you want to be valued by someone else, start by valuing yourself enough to invest time and energy in the personal presentation aspect of your Personal Resonance.

The sad reality is that people do make unfair snap judgments based on appearances. So if you're in this game of life to get the most out of it, in romance or in any other area, it's just plain smart to consider your appearance as simply one more way to influence others, and with intention. If your intention is to appear businesslike, you'll dress quite differently than you might if you're in a seductive mood. What's appropriate for a business meeting is probably not appropriate for a romantic date.

Be flexible. Be willing to change with the circumstances. Be willing to try something new. After all, everyone's watched people at the airport or the shopping mall who look as if they're not sure what decade it is. Think for a moment about what a person who's still wearing clothing or hair styles from 20 years ago says through their appearance and presentation. It might be any of several things.

Their Personal Resonance might be that they felt best about themselves 20 years ago, that they feel their best years are behind them. Is someone who feels their best years are behind them appealing to you? Maybe you like hearing tales of high school accomplishments from someone hovering at the cusp of age 40. But most people would probably prefer someone whose Personal Resonance is focused on who they are today, now who they were 20 years ago.

Wearing styles from long ago or being dismissive about grooming might also suggest a person who is afraid of change. Is that a good thing? After all, change is going to happen no matter what. Letting life happen or making life happen both work. You don't necessarily have to stay with a new change. Just try it, for the adventure alone. But perhaps embracing change, actively taking it on and directing it with focused intention, is a better approach to life, if you're interested in getting the most out of it, that is.

Not updating one's appearance and attending to one's health might also reflect a lack of creativity or self-awareness, probably not what you'd prefer if you're interested in personal growth, and growth with a Heartmate, by your side. Remember that natural law, the one about attraction? If you take care of yourself, you'll attract others who take care of themselves, meaning you won't end up with a spouse or partner who behaves more as a child, expecting you to take care of him or her.

You don't have to become a trend-following fashionista or spend thousands on your clothes. But do see if you're presenting the image you want to convey to the world. If not, have a few trusted friends, true Balance Partners, help you determine if your look is transmitting what you'd really like the world, and all those potential Heartmates, to know about you.

A shift in appearance is a shift in Personal Resonance, too. Invest in a makeover, or go shopping with a friend whose taste you admire. Gain some flexibility in your personal style. You can always go back to what you've been doing later if you like. But at least try something different. If you're feeling stuck in your life, change something over which you have control. Your appearance certainly qualifies. As you reprogram your Personal Resonance, don't forget about your personal style. It makes a huge difference in how you feel about yourself, as anyone who's struggled through a bad hair day well knows.

And if you meet a potential Heartmate who's charming and lovely, but who could use a few pointers on how to update their look or become better groomed, don't give up. Perhaps it's just habit and he or she is open to new possibilities. If not, you probably wouldn't enjoy spending time with someone who's stubborn about their long hair or their beard or their "but they're so comfortable" ratty old clothes. A stubborn, dated, or neglectful personal style might well reflect a stubborn and fixed-in-position inner life, too. And, of course, if you meet someone who's overly focused on appearances, you may discover that's because there's not much substance beneath that stylish exterior. As with most important aspects of life, flexibility and balance are important.

Soul or Mate

If you put the "mate" aspect of soulmate ahead of the soul-to-soul connection with potential heartmates, you're likely to find yourself frustrated at the people who rejected you after you'd offered yourself to them in a physically intimate way. You may feel cheated, or used. Again, don't blame yourself. Don't feel guilty. Don't convince yourself that you're unworthy of deeper connections, or that you're only valuable for what you can offer on a sexual level. None of that is true. Instead, put your focus on the soul-level learning opportunity you've just had, figure out what you learned, and then move on.

Use the moment Now to reframe your thinking about your choices, to heal your past. If you feel that you have a history of becoming sexually involved too early, instead of telling yourself, "My mother's right; I'm a slut" reframe it as, "My loving and affectionate nature led me to become sexual too soon in relationships, but Now I no longer choose to do that." Sounds a whole lot better, doesn't it? It broadcasts an entirely different Personal Resonance. An empowered, self-aware Resonance. A willingness to change.

A programming change sucha as that absolutely transforms your Heartmate connection potential. Kindness to you results in kindness from others. It's all about your Personal Resonance.

And that's entirely within your control.

Chapter 11:
The Five Big Blocks

Believing in fate produces fate. Believing in freedom will create infinite possibilities.

—Ayn Rand

Finding a Heartmate, as you already know, is a journey—sometimes a long one, but always a worthy one. One possible reason you've not yet found the Heartmate relationship you want is that you're blocking your progress with one—or more—of what I call the Five Big Blocks. Blocking your path to soulmate relationships, particularly to Heartmate bonds, isn't necessarily a conscious behavior. In fact, it's probably something you do without even realizing it. But your Personal Resonance broadcasts blocks as well as invitations in exactly the same way; it takes no position on which is "better." It simply does what you program it to do. Although soulmates of all types enrich our lives, I have found that the Five Big Blocks are most often at work in romantic soulmate relationships.

Clearly it's in your best interest to discover and remove any blocks to your relationship progress. That is, to learn how to better invite new relationship possibilities into your life, or to develop new ways of behaving within your existing relationships. To invite new relationships—or renewed relationships. To invite new love—or renewed love. To clean up the negative programming in your Personal Resonance and replace it with something that serves you better.

Almost any reason you can name for why you haven't found a Heartmate is a variation on one of the Five Big Blocks. Blocks, simply stated, are fears. What you fear, you attract. Whether or not you're in touch with your fears and blocks (and everyone has blind spots), they'll attract on that same level. They're programmed to be attractive, magnetic. They seek a similar "vibe" with which to resonate. Aware or unaware, you're broadcasting *something*.

If you're not pleased with the results you've had so far in the Heartmate department, it's time to find out what your Personal Resonance is, what you're *really* resonating. You're blocking your success on some level. You're standing in your own way. But once you know how you're doing that, you can transform your Personal Resonance to one that broadcasts, "seeking a Heartmate for lasting love."

You may not understand just yet how you're blocking yourself from attracting romantic Heartmates and helpful Balance Partners who could grow into Heartmates (or maybe introduce you to them), or why you're consistently attracting Karmic Connections that involve lots of struggles. By seeking to understand the how and the why, you're bringing these important questions to your waking awareness, your consciousness. That's the first step toward reprogramming your Personal Resonance to attract a compatible Heartmate.

The Five Big Blocks

In the next several chapters, I'll discuss these Five Big Blocks in detail, but for now, here's the short list. As you read through it, make notes of your initial gut reaction in your journal. Which ones sound the most similar to something you'd say, or have said? Which ones just seem like "truth" to you? Which ones make you laugh in understanding? Which ones give you a little "aha!" moment of awareness?

Pay attention to your responses—that's your Inner Soulmate at work, your Inner Wisdom bringing hidden negative beliefs, little bits of psychological negative programming to the surface so you can remove them and improve your life, just as you'd take spyware and malware off your computer to improve its performance.

ONE: "I'd rather be anything but alone."

This block resonates desperation. If you've ever felt that any relationship is better than no relationship, you know what this block is about. I've also seen this block, and close variations, in people who won't let go of a long relationship simply because it's a long relationship. They may continue to stay with their first love, well, because it's their first love. They feel first should mean forever. It's also common in people who've never lived alone or been fully self-sufficient before settling into a long-term relationship.

TWO: "But I see such potential."

This block resonates hope, which isn't, in itself, a bad thing; not at all. But if you've ever stayed too long with someone who was self-destructive, or physically or emotionally hurtful to you or others, in the hope they'd change, you've experienced the block that high hopes can create. Although it's wonderful that you see someone's potential—that shining soul inside a very troubled person—that individual must take responsibility, take active steps to bring their Best Self to light. They must use *their* free will, not ride along on yours. If they're not taking steps to actively achieve their potential, you're blocking yourself from happiness with a true Heartmate by staying in the relationship because you hope things will change.

THREE: "It's just that I love you so much."

This block resonates a belief that love will heal all things. And certainly, it does. But "healing" isn't "curing." You can't cure someone's lack of romantic interest in you. You can send healing love their way, asking your Inner Soulmate and theirs to send even more compassion and love to encourage a shift in their viewpoint. But true unconditional love isn't attached to an outcome. It doesn't cling. It's not jealous. You already know that clinging (and its scarier cousin, stalking) won't help bridge the gap between you. True love is never desperate. It's strong and secure in itself and its power, asking nothing in return.

FOUR: *"I won't be hurt like that again."*

This block resonates "I'm an open wound." It indicates an incomplete healing of a difficult relationship that's over. It broadcasts, "I'm a victim." This block is often found in people who aren't comfortable reflecting on their relationships to see the soul-level lessons. These are the people who tell The Story (often). And they often use that story to elicit sympathy from others. They may be manipulative through seeking sympathy or support because they've experienced many challenges in life. This block is often seen in people who avoid taking responsibility for their part in their relationships, as well as in people who use indirect methods of communication or passive aggressive behavior.

FIVE: *"All the good ones are gone."*

This block resonates that you're letting numbers rule your romantic life. Logic trumps feeling. You're letting your analytical left brain overrule your creative right brain. Demographics are a fact of life, of course. Women live longer. Men tend to date people younger than themselves. But with some creativity, and willingness to date outside your comfort zone—whether that's younger people, older people, or people of a different culture, race, or socioeconomic status—you can attract soulmates with Heartmate potential. Let go of attachments to outcomes, and enjoy the journey. Remember: All you need is one good one. Just one.

That's not such a tough assignment, is it? Not when you work from what you can control: your free will choices in the moment Now to transform your Personal Resonance. It's all about you, really.

Are you ready to face yourself? Break free from your blocks? Attract that Heartmate for lasting love? Then it's time to access your Inner Wisdom as you sort out what's blocking your progress in attracting a Heartmate bond. Read the next several chapters with your journal close by so you can jot down your *aha!* moments and insights, those clues from your Inner Soulmate.

Listen closely. You have all the information available. Ask and you shall receive insights and inspiration that can transform your life. Especially your love life.

Chapter 12:
I'd Rather Be Anything
But Alone

So one thing I want to say about life is don't be scared and don't hang back, and most of all, don't waste it.

—Joan W. Blos

Feeling lonely is something all people experience, but some people so fear that feeling that they convey an almost desperate desire to have a partner. This often leads them into relationships that they might have avoided, if their fear of being alone weren't so strong.

Often without even realizing it, people who project what I call the "I'd rather be anything but alone" block via their Personal Resonance transmit a sense of desperation, a reluctance to know themselves at a deeper level, a wariness to be self sufficient. Because like attracts like, the relationships these people attract are often unfulfilling and fear-based, comprised of partners who cling together, no matter how awful the relationship, because being alone is more frightening than staying. They can't imagine a happy life without someone else there with them. Perhaps they fear that "this is the best I can do, no one else would want me." With negative self-talk such as that, it's no wonder they stay with a known and familiar commodity: the relationship they're currently in, no matter how bad.

How do people end up in such relationships? Often from the very beginning they aren't selective in whom they allow to share their lives. It's what I call the "You like me? Then I like you!" approach to finding a Heartmate. They let themselves by defined by the *other* person's interest, never thinking to ask their Inner Wisdom for guidance in the matter. Does this feel right to me? Does it resonate with my inner being, my true essence? Those questions are important to ask in any relationship, whether with friends, colleagues, or potential lovers.

If you've been through this kind of desperately-seeing-someone relationship yourself, you know that being flattered into a relationship doesn't exactly build the rock-solid foundation you need for a long-term Heartmate relationship. And reflecting on the origins of that relationship, you probably can now see that the signs that it wasn't in your best interest to become involved were there, just overlooked.

You probably know people who block their development on a soul level by being "run" by their fear of being alone. Single people who resonate the "I'd rather be anything but alone" block are the ones who are mentally planning the wedding after the first coffee date. People already in relationships with the "I'd rather be anything but alone" block are the ones who hang on, no matter what their partner does, often tolerating infidelities, addictions, or even emotional or physical abuse. Their panic leads them to overlook far too much, far too often. To help understand and eradicate that fear, many people find that professional counseling helps strengthen their resolve and become more comfortable with themselves, reducing the desperation that attracts people who help them learn, but in difficult and challenging ways.

Moving slowly, consulting your Inner Wisdom as you attract soulmates who may be Heartmates (or who could evolve with you into Heartmate status), may seem to be a waste of time when you're in your late 30s and wondering if you'll ever become a parent. But it's *spiritually efficient* to take your time, to move slowly, to trust your insights, to ask your Inner Wisdom for guidance. On a soul level, time isn't even real so take all you need to make wise decisions.

Remember: Feeling an instant attraction, doesn't mean you must make an instant decision. The wise course usually is the one that you come to gradually, gently. Trust your higher self, your Inner Wisdom. Your soul's not in a hurry to connect: That's your human ego, your human self, panicking. Your soul's eternal after all, and eternity lasts a long time. Relax. Slow down. Focus on attracting a Heartmate, a soulmate with whom you can share a romantic life, and not on a human timeline measured in days, months and years.

Variations on Theme

Here are some variations strongly correlated with the "I'd rather be anything but alone" Resonance Pattern. See if any of the following statements ring true for you as you look over your relationship history and your current (or most recent) romantic relationship. If they do, take time to journal about them, mull them over, and consider what you'd like to program into your Persona Resonance broadcast instead to attract a lasting Heartmate bond.

"If I didn't do all these things for him, he'd leave me."

Beneath this statement is the fear of abandonment. If you're involved with someone who counts on you to handle of mundane tasks of life that ideally should be shared, such as cooking, cleaning, entertaining, and managing the home, and feel that if you weren't there everything would fall apart, you're wrong. That's simply not true. He'd cook more or become a junk-food junkie perhaps, live in a messier house maybe, but he wouldn't be unable to manage. He'd cope. You're not indispensable. Ask yourself whether you are valued more for what you do than for who you are.

"If I don't do all these things for my kids, people will say I'm a bad parent."

Fear of failure, of being judged by others, is behind this one. So what if the neighbors think your kid should have a neater room? Or have a chauffeured ride home from school instead of taking the bus? You need time to yourself, to listen to your soul's call, to hear that inner voice, your Inner Wisdom. To replenish your energy at a soul level so you can then add that powerful soulmate energy to any relationship. Your kids can learn to pick up their rooms, to make their beds, to take the school bus home. These changes also encourage self-reliance, which is an added bonus. Look for areas in your life from which you can take 10 to 15 minutes a day. You can find them. And don't feel guilty about "stealing" time from others, or from mundane tasks such as cleaning the house. You're not stealing time; you're investing time in *you.*

Fear that time is running out.

"If I don't meet someone in the next year, I'll never have children of my own." A ticking biological clock is real for many people, particularly women oler than 35 who wish to be parents. But resonating "I'd like you to be the father of my children" right from the start only scares men away. They can "smell" your assessment of them as a potential "baby daddy" from that first phone call or e-mail exchange. It's more spiritually efficient to first match up on the soulmate resonance level, and then worry about bringing kids into the bond.

"I can't make it on my own financially."

Fear of financial self-reliance is a huge issue for many people. It's a fact of life: Most people have to work. Economics matter. But are you willing to trade off your personal happiness to stay in a relationship that has as its number-one attraction a bit of financial security? And these days, economic security isn't assured for anyone. How many people do you know who lost a pension they'd counted on, for example? Remember Enron?

The wise move is to plan for your economic self-reliance no matter the state of your romantic relationships. If you're not yet married or partnered, finish your education first. This will allow you to make decisions based on what (and who) feeds your soul, not what or who pays your bills. If you are married or partnered, and want to pursue an education now, find a way. No excuses: Today there are more options than ever before.

There are Internet training programs. Take one class at a time. So what if it takes three years instead of two to finish. That's okay. You can find a way to create the financial wherewithal to go to school. There are scholarships. There are grants. There are loans. And there is learning the difference between *need* and *want.* You only *need* three or four pairs of shoes, not 23. Cars can last eight to

10 years, or more. You don't *need* a new one; you *want* a new one. Once you sort out what you need from what you want, you'll realize that you can have four or more years without car payments. Better to take a loan on the investment in *you*, a loan for your education, than on a car.

Finances do matter. But are you essentially exchanging your soul-level happiness for stuff to stay in a relationship that doesn't make you happy where it really counts, in your heart? Here's how to tell. If you can answer "yes" to the question, "If you had a few million dollars in the bank just waiting, would you leave your relationship?" you already know what your Inner Wisdom is trying to guide you toward. The rest is a matter of sorting out details.

Where It Comes From

Jot down your reactions in your journal as you read through the following possible reasons as the root of the "I'd rather be anything but alone" block. Pay particular attention to those that seem to hit home, to resonate deeply. You may not have had exactly the experiences outlined here, but trust your Inner Wisdom to provide messages to you through your physical and emotional reactions. Pay attention if you react strongly to any of these situations or suddenly recall an event from your own life as you read through them.

Holding on by doing for.

By nurturing others, on some level (not necessarily a conscious one), people may have the expectation that their efforts to make others happy will keep them attached. Sometimes called the "disease to please," this behavior often backfires because others come to expect it as a given.

A need for appreciation.

Just being themselves feels as if it's not enough for some people. Praise for doing, rather than praise for simply being, leads many people to continually seek approval. External valuation often leads to a desire for high levels of achievement. That's not necessarily bad. But if you know people who'd become unhinged at the thought of a

B grade, or who fear a not-so-terrific work review (at a job they don't even especially like) may ruin their careers, you can see how this fear of failure can lay the foundation for a fear of being alone, particularly if being single is considered a failure on some level.

Physical loss of a parent or parental figure.

Whether it's to adoption, death, or divorce, or because you never knew a parent (such as a sperm-donor pregnancy or when the father of the child disappears or is never told of the pregnancy), the early loss of a parent or other influential figure in childhood often establishes the foundational conditions that lead to fear of abandonment. This is particularly true if you were very young, under age 6 or 7, when the loss occurred. Often people who've been through such big losses cling to others, particularly romantic soulmates, even if the relationships are unhealthy.

Emotional loss of an influential figure.

If you were raised in an unsupportive home environment in which a parent or influential adult figure struggled with an addiction, or who lived with an emotional or mental disorder that made day-to-day life unpredictable, you may grow up to fear change and loss to a greater degree than others. The emotional rug is pulled out from under children in such circumstances, who must learn to fend for themselves emotionally, long before they're really ready to do so. A fear of being alone and without support in adulthood isn't surprising in people who've already been there, done that as children.

Moving often.

If the working members of your family were in the military or had other life circumstances that required geographical moves often during your childhood, the uncertainty in your physical home environment may also have set up the foundation for the "I'd rather be anything but alone" Resonance Pattern. This is also true if you lived in foster care or moved around among extended family members to live with.

Are You Resonating "I'd Rather Be Anything But Alone"?

My daily environment as a child was unpredictable. If you have an instinctual reaction to that statement, take some time to discover whether you are broadcasting the "I'd rather be anything but alone" Resonance Pattern, which is getting in the way of your ability to attract an appropriate Heartmate bond, a positive one. Remember: Soulmates are living lessons, people with whom you have an affiliation, so you may as well attract joyful lessons and affiliations, not painful ones. Haven't you had enough of those already?

Here's a self-assessment to help you discover whether you may be resonating the "I'd rather be anything but alone" block. Answer the following statements by choosing a number from 1 to 5, based on how strongly you agree with it. Five means it fits you completely; one means it's not descriptive of you at all. You may find that retaking this self-assessment later will show quite different results. That's great; that's evidence that you're making personal transformations.

Take notes in your journal as you take this for the first time so that you have a baseline self-assessment to refer to later, particularly when you're feeling impatient or that you're not seeing the results you want. But, as you know by now, being too attached to a particular outcome actually works against you. Focus on the voice of your own soul, the energy, the vibe, and on what you wish to attract my changing your Personal Resonance Pattern.

Resonance Self-Assessment:

The "I'd rather be anything but alone" Resonance Pattern

1. I've never liked being alone. 1 2 3 4 5

2. If I had a day with nothing planned, I'd try to spend it with others. 1 2 3 4 5

3. I've never been without a romantic interest for very long. 1 2 3 4 5

4. When I try to meditate or just "do nothing" I fidget; I can't sit still. 1 2 3 4 5

5. I tend to stay in familiar situations with friendships, work, and romance even when I know it's in my best interest to leave. 1 2 3 4 5

6. If I were to look at a recent "to-do list" I made, things that I do for others which they could do for themselves but don't are at the top. 1 2 3 4 5

7. The opinions of others matter a great deal to me, even if they're people I don't even know. 1 2 3 4 5

8. When I take a break just for myself, I feel guilty. 1 2 3 4 5

Total: "I'd rather be anything but alone" pattern:_____

Score: Interpretation:

32 to 40   You have strong elements of this Resonance Pattern on a regular basis; it's a major block for you to clear.

24 to 31   You show aspects of this pattern; it's a potential block to which you should pay attention.

15 to 23   This is an occasional Resonance Pattern for you.

14 or less This Resonance Pattern isn't a block for you.

Releasing the Block Through Focusing on You

If you're broadcasting the "I'd rather be anything but alone" Resonance Pattern, or one of the variations previously noted, you can turn it around. Even when it's difficult, even when it hurts, and particularly when you begin to feel guilty about spending too much time on yourself (this is that "disease to please" again), remember that everything that you're doing for yourself eventually is reflected back to you through others. It's that spiritual efficiency at work, that Law of Karma.

Don't play small with your energy. Don't give so much of yourself away that you disappear from your own life. Investing time and energy in self development is actually investing in your future Heartmate. That applies even if you're working on the relationship you're in now, working to elevate it to a true Heartmate bond.

Here's to freeing yourself from fear, to releasing limiting blocks, to investing in yourself, to reprogramming your Personal Resonance, and to attracting a Heartmate.

Take the risk. The reward is love. And that's worth changing for.

Chapter 13:
But I See Such Potential

When we are no longer able to change a situation we are challenged to change ourselves.

—*Viktor Frankl*

If you've ever fallen for someone based on who you think they could become, or stayed in a relationship because once upon a time things were great, you may be what I call a potential junkie, someone who says "but I know he/she can change." Yes, it's true, he or she can. But will he? That's an entirely different question. That goes to his actual level of motivation, not your dream or your fantasy about his motivation. You're dealing with what I call the "But I see such potential" block.

If you were ever involved with someone whom trusted friends and family members consistently felt was simply not worthy of you, who wasn't yet showing the world what I call his Best Self, chances are that you were falling for someone's potential. You were hooked on who someone said they would become. Might grow into. Wish they were. Maybe used to be. You were living in a fantasy world.

This block to true Heartmate relationship success is particularly common in the wild world of Internet dating. There, who you really are and who you *say* you really are can be (and often are) completely different. Because of the divergence between truth and tale so often found there (and some studies show that about 2/3 of people on some sites are actually married), people who say they're in love with someone they know only from their online encounters are most often potential junkies. They're not falling in love; they're falling for the fantasy.

That's because relationships in which you aren't up close and personal on a regular basis are essentially fantasies. When you're not together, you quite naturally "fill in the blanks" and create a vision of who you think the other person is, or would like them to be. You then are able to breeze right past any number of red flags that, under other circumstances, would warn you to pay closer attention. Chemistry with someone else is powerful, but, fantasy world you create yourself is often even more powerful.

Slow Down, You Move Too Fast

Slow down. Don't be tempted to become a potential junkie by not paying enough attention or moving too fast at the outset of a relationship. And although it's true that sometimes people meet, have a whirlwind romance, and stay married for the next 45 years, most too-much-too-soon romances don't work out well.

How many people do you know who ended up in long-term relationships with people they had short flings or one night stands with? Whatever the number, it's much smaller than the number of long-term relationships between people who took their time. Being optimistic is one thing, but being delusional and seeing potential where there is none is entirely another.

Striking a balance between hopeful anticipation and realistic groundedness isn't easy, of course. But it's important that you strive to achieve that balance if you want to have a long-lasting romantic soulmate partnership with a Heartmate.

Instant Insight

As much as I tout intuition, literally your "inner teacher," relying *solely* on your natural intuition is unwise when it comes to relationships. When you meet new people, particularly those you may have a romantic interest in, expand on your initial impressions with logical reasoning and structured assessment. Add the view of your head to the insight of your heart. Record your initial impressions as soon after meeting, even if it's an online introduction. Keep that information close by as the relationship evolves.

Later, when you're troubled or confused about something within the relationship, refer to those notes from your initial encounters. You're likely to be surprised at how much you missed. You may discover many red flags you breezed right by that allowed your attachment to a person's potential, or the sexual chemistry between you, to influence you more than it should have.

Certainly there are times when you may choose to overlook something because you are more afraid of the difficulty of ending the relationship, or of being alone. Deep down, if you're honest with yourself, you know there are red flags, possibly even some very big red flags. Still, you elect to go stay in the relationship anyway.

Why the inertia? On some level, you are still focused on the potential of the relationship. You're focused on What Used To Be, or What Might Be, not What Is. You're counting on re-creating the past or transforming the future. You're not living in the moment, in the truth of What Is Now. In many ways, a "But I see such potential" relationship is a very lonely kind of relationship to be involved in because you can't connect in the moment Now if you prefer to live in the past or the future.

When to Bail Out

How do you know when to give up hoping for change? That someone will begin to realize that wonderful potential? If you aren't seeing steps in the direction of self responsibility from the other party within a reasonable time frame, move on. Yes, that means you may have to put some distance between you and someone you love very much. But how much do you want a truly rewarding partnership, a deeply loving and supportive Heartmate bond? If you really want that sustained soulmate relationship, a true Heartmate connection in which you feel treasured, loved, and desired on all levels—body, mind, spirit, and soul—moving on is often the best move you can make.

In fact, sometimes making a move toward moving on rekindles the romance you thought you were leaving. It can actually trigger that promised potential to become in-the-moment-Now action. You may find that your partner rises to the challenge. The clarity that emerges when you really leave, with no intention of returning, is often a catalyst for improvement. Just be careful not to say you're leaving until you're actually able to do it without looking back. Otherwise, you could become one of those couples who attempt to break up several times before they actually manage to do it.

Who's Doing the Work Here?

If your Personal Resonance attracts people who aren't motivated to work on themselves, much of the work within the relationship will fall on your shoulders. If there's to be growth, you'll have to start it, and maintain it. If you sense that someone you're interested in as a romantic soulmate (or even from someone you've been involved with for many years) is perfectly happy to stay right where they are, who has no particular interest in self-growth and development through a hobby, volunteer work, educational classes, or something other than their work or business life, I encourage you to think about what they're really telling you, which is, "I'm not interested in bettering myself."

Because we're here in human form to learn and to grow, I consider this a form of emotional and spiritual laziness. Why waste the opportunity for personal growth? If you've ever heard from a romantic soulmate "but you knew what you were getting into" or "you knew who I was from the beginning," you know what this really means is, "I won't change. I won't. I won't." It's childish stubbornness, an unwillingness to bend—a form of laziness.

Because change is inevitable, you may as well seek out a Heartmate who's interested in thriving, not just surviving. Who's interested in bending in your direction at least some of the time. Thriving includes embracing the highest and best possibilities on body, mind, spirit, and soul levels. Thriving is living from your Inner Wisdom, from your soul.

If you want to thrive, you'll have to live in the Now. Being a potential junkie, focused on what might be, doesn't serve you when it comes to living full out, to thriving, in the moment, Now.

Close Cousins: I Can't Hear You

A close cousin of "But I see such potential" Personal Resonance block is the "I can't hear you" block. The "I can't hear you" vibe is akin to a child sticking his fingers in his ears, squinting his eyes, and pretending things that he doesn't like aren't really there. It's a form of denial, of putting the best face on things. You can also think of it as the, "I don't want to face the truth" resonance pattern.

Facing the truth is never easy. But pretending something problematic doesn't even exist, or creating a fantasy relationship based on a very shaky foundation—something many people who meet online are prone to doing—doesn't serve you either on that all-important soul level. If you're honest with yourself, it probably hasn't worked very well in practical terms in your life, either. Your Inner Wisdom would be telling you that very same thing, if you didn't have your fingers in your ears, eyes squinted, saying (energetically at least), "I can't hear you."

Where It Comes From

Underneath the "But I see such potential" block is a deep fear of being hurt by acknowledging a dangerous or unhealthy situation. By noticing the elephant in the living room instead of continuing to walk around it, you are putting life as you know it at risk. Acknowledging something begins the process of transforming it, of changing it. Free will means you can't say for sure what will happen, and being unable to predict an outcome is uncomfortable. So inertia sets in. You stay with the known commodity and put the best face on it.

Here are three situations that can plant the seeds of the "I can't hear you" resonance pattern which blocks your ability to attract a Heartmate with whom you could be joyful and content. Jot down your reactions in your journal as you read through them. Pay particular attention to those that strike you quite strongly, and to any memories that arise.

Living in fearful circumstances.

If you grew up in a situation in which you lived in fear, where violence, abuse, or the threat of violence or abuse was a typical event, you may have learned to cope through denying the depth of the situation. As a child, of course, you had very little power to change things. Denying the truth worked; it was necessary for your survival not to look deeply into the situation. But that was then, and this is Now. In the moment Now, as an adult with many more options and much more personal power, facing the truth of your life both past and present is the secret to a transformed—and happier—future.

Talking so that you don't have to listen.

Many people, particularly women, use nervous talking as a cover-up for fear, so that they don't have to listen to what's really being communicated. Keeping in mind that more than 3/4 of communication is nonverbal, talking doesn't really communicate as much as you think it does. And by talking too much, you don't have to listen as closely. Which allows you to continue to live in the fantasy of who someone might be rather than who he actually is.

If you've ever been through an abrupt breakup during which the other person insisted, "But I've been telling you for six months that we have problems and you simply didn't listen," you may have been broadcasting the "I can't hear you" resonance pattern to avoid dealing with the problems. Facing the truth about someone else also means facing the truth about yourself. Never easy, but always worth the effort.

Being overly optimistic.

Being positive is a good thing. Being unrealistically positive, not seeing a situation for what it actually is, is not. If you've ever witnessed someone cope amazingly well in a crisis, perhaps the death of a loved one, only to break down weeks, months, or even years later, you've witnessed the power of positive thinking to defer feelings of intense grief.

Many times, a seemingly unrelated or less significant event triggers overwhelming sadness. Someone who lost both parents in a tragic car accident, for example manages to reach adulthood appearing to have adjusted quite nicely. Then, a breakup with a lover, the loss of a job, the death of a pet, or any other grief-inducing incident unleashes a 20-years-in-the-making torrent of sadness. Again, as a child your resources were much more limited. But as an adult you have the power to reframe things, Now.

Invisible Me

Sometimes I feel that I'm invisible, that nobody even notices me. If you have an instinctual reaction to that statement, take some time to discover whether you are broadcasting the "I can't hear you" Resonance Pattern, which is getting in the way of your ability to attract an appropriate soulmate. Remember: Soulmates are living lessons, people with whom you have an affiliation, so you may as well attract joyful lessons and affiliations, not painful ones. Haven't you had enough of those already?

Here's a self-assessment that you can take to see if you may be broadcasting the "But I see such potential" Resonance Pattern or its variations. Answer the following statements by choosing a number from 1 to 5, based on how strongly you agree with it. Five means it fits you completely; one means it's not descriptive of you at all. You may find that retaking this self-assessment later will show quite different results. That's great; that's evidence that you're making personal transformations.

You may wish to take notes in your journal so that you have a baseline self-assessment that includes your feelings, not just your numerical responses to refer to later, particularly when you're feeling impatient or that you're not seeing the results you want. But as you know by now, being too attached to a particular outcome actually works against you. Focus on the soul, the energy, the vibe, a Resonance Pattern that you wish to attract my changing your own.

Resonance Self-Assessment:

The "But I See Such Potential" Resonance Pattern

1. I've always looked on the bright side. 1 2 3 4 5

2. People tell me that I don't always see people's true motives. 1 2 3 4 5

3. I've always enjoyed novels and movies with happy endings more than other types of books, even though I know they're fantasies. 1 2 3 4 5

4. I like to take people at their word so I don't usually challenge statements they make. 1 2 3 4 5

5. When I think about a former love relationship that ended, I usually don't recall how hurt I was. 1 2 3 4 5

6. I'm always surprised when I discover people haven't told me the whole story about something. 1 2 3 4 5

7. I find that usually I'm the peacemaker among feuding family members, coworkers, or friends. 1 2 3 4 5

8. I'm the cheerleader, the one who always gives others lots of positive support, among my family, friends, and coworkers. 1 2 3 4 5

Total: "But I See Such Potential" pattern:_____

Score:	Interpretation:
32 to 40	You have strong elements of this Resonance pattern on a regular basis; it's a major block for you to clear.
24 to 31	You show aspects of this pattern; it's a potential block to which you should pay attention.
15 to 23	This is an occasional Resonance pattern for you.
14 or less	This Resonance pattern isn't a block for you.

Ask for guidance as you work on releasing the "But I see such potential" block from your Personal Resonance. Your Inner Wisdom will assist you as reach out energetically and send out a call for a Heartmate to love and be loved by. Listen to your Inner Soulmate, that aspect of your Inner Wisdom that focuses on relationships, and there's no need to get hung up on someone's potential.

That's because you'll be dealing with a beautiful reality, a balanced and happy What Is and, soon, attracting a Heartmate relationship courtesy of your powerful partnership with your Inner Wisdom.

Chapter 14:
It's Just That I Love You So Much

The way to love anything is to realize that it might be lost.

—*G. K. Chesterton*

If a great deal of love is intensely focused on someone, it can actually block your progress in attracting a healthy Heartmate bond, or improving the one you have already. This seems illogical, yet it can be true. You *can* "love too much" in the sense that too much of a good thing feels overwhelming to the other person. This is what I call the "It's just that I love you so much" Resonance pattern.

Extending your love to someone seems to be a completely natural and welcome act, which it certainly is. But when you love someone with such intensity and force that they feel smothered, overwhelmed, or unable to breathe (emotionally speaking, anyway) the power of your Personal Resonance is actually pushing them away, not bringing them closer. That's not what you're hoping for when you're seeking a long-term life partner, a true Heartmate.

Even when wrapped in the attractive paper of grand romantic gestures and evident concern for the well-being of the other person, "It's just that I love you so much" is often a form of subtle, even manipulative, control. When you care about someone so deeply that they occupy your mind to the point where following them, checking their e-mail, calling or texting them several or even dozens of times a day seems logical, you're actually blocking your soul development (and theirs, too). Things are out of balance. Loving someone too much puts that person higher on your priority list than your own personal development, particularly on the soul level.

Because the whole point of life on earth is to develop as a soul, putting yourself at the top of your priority list is the wisest thing you can do. Actually, that's what your Inner Wisdom is guiding you toward, always: the most fulfilling experiences, particularly those that include your soulmates—Karmic Connections, Balance Partners, and especially Heartmates.

If you've ever been on the receiving end of this kind of devoted, perhaps even unwelcome but "loving" attention, you know that there's a fine line between being loved and practically being stalked by someone. At first, you may feel flattered at all the attention. But eventually, it starts to dawn on you: Something's not quite right. The situation feels out of balance. You begin to wonder if the other person has no life. How is it that he or she has the time to write 14 e-mails, text you 39 times, and call you several times a day, too? If you're the one lavishing too much interest on the other person in the early stages of a fledgling relationship, you are doing exactly the same thing: pushing the object of your interest away through too much intensity.

For many people, pulling back when they are first getting to know someone in whom they're very interested is extremely difficult. It's exciting to feel that strong initial attraction, to find your thoughts occupied with a new love interest, a potential Heartmate. That excitement is a good sign, but it's also why, as a general rule, it's best to move slowly from the very beginning. Speed can be dangerous. It's easier to slow a car moving 15 miles an hour than one moving 50.

Be especially careful if you're a dating Website regular. Even if you've spent hours online or on the telephone, by the time you actually meet in person, keep your first in-person encounter short. Spending four hours on a first date with someone who's essentially a total stranger resonates an almost desperate interest. It appears to that person that perhaps you don't have an interesting, engaging life of you own. Maybe you don't. But you should. Develop your own interests, get involved in your own life and you'll soon find that potential romantic soulmates find you much more interesting. Desperation is rarely attractive.

Relationships, particularly romantic ones, rank among the greatest delights in life. That's why it's tempting to spend hours together on a first date. There's that pesky potential again: "This could be The One." But if you're relying on other people to complete your life and fill your days, you're missing out. Instead, seek a romantic soulmate who will enhance your life, better your life, share your life—but not complete your life.

It's your job to live your life to the fullest extent possible. Loving someone too much too soon truncates that possibility: You find his or her life more interesting than your own. You live vicariously through him or her to some degree, allowing the excitement in his or her life to fill in the gaps in your own. That's not balanced or healthy on any level, especially on the soul level.

It's a Numbers Game

If you're dating again after a long period, be careful not to focus solely on one potential romantic soulmate possibility. You're here to learn as much as you can through experience and relationships. The more experiences in the more relationships (whether with Karmic Connections, Balance Partners, Heartmates), with friends, colleagues, or family members, the better for your soul.

This is especially true during those times when you're coming off a breakup, a divorce, or some other painful ending to a relationship. Realize that the next several romantic involvements you have probably will represent adjustment relationships. You're not yet completely clear or completely healed, so you will naturally be resonating that lack of clarity.

That's fine, it's perfectly normal. But once you're aware of your vulnerability because of that lack of clarity, move slowly. If you've been with someone for longer than two years, give yourself at least a year between serious involvements to learn, to heal, to understand, and mostly to clarify what you want. Be gentle with yourself. Move slowly.

That doesn't mean you shouldn't get out there and date. Just have fun. Keep it light. Think of each one of those next two or three or four short relationships as a step on the path that leads to the ideal

Heartmate for the person you are Now. Learn from each one and ask your Inner Wisdom for guidance. Pay attention to the insights you receive.

If you pay attention, you'll soon learn that people tell you who they are very early. Listen carefully from that deep intuitive Knowing. Notice what people tell you, as well as what they don't. Hesitation or ambivalence can be particularly confusing. Always consider hesitation to mean "no." Very often, the other person simply doesn't want to tell you the truth, afraid you'll be hurt.

If there is a mistake people make in seeking a Heartmate, it's not paying attention to these signs early on. "I'm not sure" means "no." An evasive or delayed response to "Are you seriously involved with anyone else right now?" means "no." You'll save yourself a lot of heartache by remembering that ambivalence and hesitation are as important to listen to as the next words that follow.

Don't Go Overboard

When you approach the level of becoming obsessed with someone else, or become the object of someone else's near obsession, it's time to step back and assess the situation. Obsession isn't interesting. Obsession is off-putting, and at times even scary. Finding a way to extend your love to someone without also extending desperation or neediness sometimes requires a lot of inner work.

If you've been hurt in your romantic encounters, and who hasn't been, of course you're fearful of being hurt. But is being hesitant and fearful helping you get what you want? Has loving someone with desperation, with the fear you might lose them foremost in mind, worked out for you? Probably not. More likely your obsession and jealousy pushed someone whom you cared about away rather than drawing them closer.

Think of the process of developing a long-term Heartmate bond in the same way that Thomas Edison invented the light bulb: He failed hundreds of times. He found a few not-quite-right-but-workable solutions somewhere along the way. He kept pressing on for something even better because he learned from each attempt. He knew he was on the right track.

As are you. Hold that awareness clearly in mind. It will transform the light that you shine, that Personal Resonance that broadcasts who you are right Now in this moment to the universe of potential soulmates. Clarity out brings clarity back. Be clear, and trust the process.

Learning to develop this kind of soul-level balance and clear awareness of your words and your value as a person is a process and sometimes a lengthy one. Give yourself time. Not every romantic relationship has long-term potential, but every relationship has learning potential. Don't avoid wonderful learning opportunities along the way. Remember Thomas Edison and his experiments, and keep at it.

Just be careful not to mix up an "I'm supposed to learn here" relationship with an "I'm supposed to keep this one" relationship. Your Inner Wisdom will help you decide which is which. Listen to it. When you look back at your relationship history chances are you can see times when you went against the wise counsel of your inner guidance.

Love Less, Hurt Less?

Loving less intensley doesn't mean that you won't hurt emotionally when relationships end. Of course you will. It's part of the game of life, the nature of human relationships. Pain is simply part of the process. But by not loving *obsessively*, by not "loving too much too soon," you actually *gain* strength as well as reduce some of the emotional pain.

Conquering your tendency to love too much too soon (or loving so much you can't let go) actually reduces your risk of being hurt again in the future. It increases your chances of receiving the kind of healthy, supportive, reciprocal love you want to experience. Slowing things down and experiencing life moment by moment, with conscious awareness, will benefit you by allowing you to notice earlier on what the lesson plan is—or how to get the lesson and then let go gracefully when it's over. And whatever the lesson, balance is part of it.

The Benefits of Balance

Too much intensity, too much obsession, too much focus on the other party (or from the other party) leads to an energetically top-heavy situation within the relationship. When you love someone to the exclusion of yourself, you're out of balance. Eventually, you'll find yourself feeling energetically depleted because it's draining you to continue to send out energy, to shine love toward another person, without receiving an equally replenishing amount in return. The energetic system, the dynamic between the two of you, backs up, blocks up, and maybe even breaks up.

A single argument becomes the proverbial last straw. A perfectly happy marriage suddenly cracks irrevocably, seemingly without warning. A man or woman comes home to find that their spouse left a note saying, "I'm leaving, you'll be hearing from the attorney soon." The stunned spouse tells friends and family members, "I don't know what happened. It's just that I loved him... So much... I can't understand why he didn't see that."

Where it Comes From

Underneath the "It's just that I love you so much" Resonance pattern you'll often find a feeling of personal inadequacy. Someone who didn't feel loved early in life, who developed the idea that they simply weren't lovable as a result, may become too attached, too invested, basically just too much in romantic soulmate relationships. In a word, obsessed.

The experience of not enough love becomes a drive to love people so much that they can't be ignored or overlooked. Love is a good thing, no question. But too much loving intensity overwhelms, smothers—floods the field, drowns the plants. On the other end of the spectrum, not enough love dries up the field, starving the plants. Either way, the situation is out of balance.

But Never 50/50

Rarely is anything equally split into a 50/50 partnership. And though it's nice to think that every relationship is in ideal balance, that both parties contribute equally in terms of their love and commitment, it just doesn't happen that way. It's the goal, not the everyday state of being. In every relationship, one person gives more than 50 percent at times. At other times, the other party in the relationship invests at a higher level. It's the natural order of things. Just as with an infinity symbol extends itself and never stops so long as both loops (input and output) are in equal proportion, a relationship can continue indefinitely also. The key is to strive for balance. Even if it's elusive and ever-changing (which it is), the goal of a 50/50 partnership held in mind programs your Personal Resonance in a way that will attract a more equally balanced Heartmate relationship. If you're putting more into a relationship than you're getting out, maybe it's time to, well, get out. Here is a self-assessment you can use to decide if you're broadcasting the "It's just that I love you so much" resonance pattern.

Resonance Self-Assessment:

The "It's just that I love you so much" Resonance Pattern

1. When I love someone, I want to do everything I can to make life easier for them even if it means I have to make sacrifices. 1 2 3 4 5

2. I send more e-mail, cards, notes, and little gifts to people I love than most people I know. 1 2 3 4 5

3. I've been told I fall in love too fast by several friends and family members. 1 2 3 4 5

4. I notice that when my relationships have ended, they've said they just didn't love me as much as I loved them, or that they felt trapped, smothered, or controlled by me. 1 2 3 4 5

5. I guess you could say I've been known to "stalk" a little when I love someone—I've gone through e-mails, cell phone call logs, and so on. 1 2 3 4 5

6. If I were to think about how many times I say "I love you" to someone I broke off with (or am involved with now), I see it was (or is) far more than I heard (or hear) back. 1 2 3 4 5

7. I'm usually the first one to declare my feelings in a romantic relationship, the first one to use the "L word." 1 2 3 4 5

8. I believe in love at first sight, and/or that you can love someone you've never met in person. 1 2 3 4 5

Total: "It's Just That I Love You So Much" pattern:_____

Score: Interpretation:

32 to 40   You have strong elements of this resonance pattern on a regular basis; it's a major block for you to clear.

23 to 31   You show aspects of this pattern; it's a potential block to which you should pay attention.

15 to 23   This is an occasional resonance pattern for you.

14 or less   This resonance pattern isn't a block for you.

As you continue toward attracting the ideal Heartmate for you at this stage of your life and your soul development, be sure to shine your love out like a beacon of light. But remember: Keep it in balance.

Send as much back to yourself as you shine out to the world. You deserve love, too. And just as like attracts like, self love starts the process of being loved by others—like Heartmates.

Chapter 15:
I Won't Be Hurt Like That Again

The day came when the risk to remain closed in a bud became more painful than the risk it took to blossom.

—Anaïs Nin

It's a natural human tendency to seek pleasure and avoid pain. When it comes to soulmate relationships, particularly romantic ones and especially when they end, the emotional pain can be so overwhelming that many people decide that they won't risk it again. You've probably declared it yourself at some time in your life: "I won't be hurt like that again." Maybe you've even decided to avoid romantic involvements entirely, focusing instead on your career interests, educational or creative pursuits, or children. All those areas of life are important.

But if you're putting your energy in those areas to avoid being hurt in the romantic arena, the first step toward reprogramming your vibe and clearing blocks to better attract your Heartmate is to be honest with yourself. Are you sitting on the sidelines?

Will I Ever Meet My Soulmate?

In my work as an intuitive consultant, I've met hundreds of people who have spent months, years, and some even decades with no romantic soulmate interactions. Many swore they weren't interested, yet one of the most commonly asked questions, even by the people who had decided to sit on the sidelines in the game of romance, was "Will I find my soulmate?" On some level, they wanted profoundly satisfying romantic relationship, a true Heartmate bond, but their Resonance Pattern was "I won't be hurt like that again."

The answer to "Will I ever find my soulmate?" is yes. You can't avoid soulmates. Karmic Connections, Balance Partners, and potential Heartmates are everywhere. But you can refuse to engage with them when your Inner Wisdom, in conjunction with the Universe, brings you opportunities. And many people do avoid dealing with romantic Heartmate love, largely because there are a few important conditions attached. First, you have to invest yourself fully for the process to work. And second, you have to let go of any preconceived notions about your romantic soulmate.

Keep in mind that you may not experience instant sexual attraction with someone who could grow into an ideal romantic soulmate, a true Heartmate for you. You may grow slowly into Heartmate status after being friends or months or even years. He or she may be from a different area than you are, or may be shorter, taller, thinner, younger, older, heavier, or balder than you imagined. He or she may even be married or otherwise unavailable (which presents you with even more decisions with which your Inner Soulmate will help you, if you ask). Sometimes the challenge is to wait for your soulmate (tip: If he's in jail while you're waiting, consult your Inner Wisdom again.), while also not giving up on other possibilities.

Here's an example. Let's say you meet someone at work whom you instantly click with emotionally and intellectually. Through time you find that sexual attraction is part of the mix. Do you start an affair which will certainly change your lives, but also the lives of others closely associated with you? Or, do you change your lives first, let go of existing attachments and seek divorces, maybe new jobs, and then become romantically involved? Do you go for it? Wait? Or forego the opportunity? Or find a way to keep a hands-off-for-now friendship?

Ah, but it's a soulmate: What do you do? There's no easy answer. Any one of those options might be the ideal answer at a given time. Consult your Inner Wisdom. Take your time deciding. Very few things in life require instant reactions, and those that do are usually related to your physical well being—such as those times when you're bleeding profusely or have to call 911.

So there's no big rush: If it's a true Heartmate connection with real staying power, taking weeks or months to decide isn't going to change anything long-term. Be grateful that you can recognize the opportunity for what it is, and take your time deciding what to do. Soulmate isn't code for "problem free."

Where It Comes From

One of the biggest factors in whether you resonate the "I won't be hurt like that again" block is associated with how the influential adults in your life viewed your first few romances. Parents who didn't approve of your first love because of the other person's family, religion, race, or some other factor often create the conditions that later allow the "I won't be hurt like that again" block to flourish. The entire affair is based on subterfuge and lies, and has the added drama of forbidden love. And when it ends, for reasons of both first love and big drama, it hurts—a lot. That pain leaves a big impact.

Of course many people choose their first soulmate romance partners precisely because they know, on some deeper level, that this will irritate a parent, who's usually also a soulmate. Generally these motivations aren't conscious, but they still operate. Listen to your inner voice to discern whether it was potential irritation toward a parent, or true love that distinguished that first relationship.

Another reason many people put up the "I won't be hurt like that again" block has to do with sexual trauma. If you were ever raped, whether by a stranger or someone you knew (date raped), were involved with someone who was emotionally or physically abusive, or experienced sexual abuse as a child, you may be understandably wary of sexual situations. These traumatic situations heal best with the help of an appropriately trained psychotherapist or counselor.

Many people resist getting help because they feel that the past is the past and it can't be changed. I agree that the past is past, on one level. On another level, I know that you can change your viewpoint, Now. And yes, the other person is the one who has the bigger problem. So the "but why should I go to counseling?" refrain is one I understand.

Refusing to deal with the pain of that past event (by facing it and clearing it from your Personal Resonance) means it runs you even in this moment Now. Take back your power. Get help if you've been traumatized sexually. You'll find a freedom you never knew was possible if you the right kind of support. (See the Resources section for some suggestions.)

Finally, the feeling of betrayal is perhaps the thing that most commonly leads to the "I won't be hurt like that again" Resonance pattern. Whether you were duped by someone who had eyes on you for some other reason, financial status, or the desire to have a step-parent (or a child), for example, or were cheated on by someone who wouldn't admit it even when directly questioned, that feeling of betrayal, of knowing you were right but not heard, leaves an ache that can stay with you for a very long time. It often becomes bitterness. You probably know someone who still carries anger so strong that when listening to them discuss an ex, you'd think it was just two months ago, not five years ago that the relationship ended.

Again, wounds of this type often heal best with the support of a trained and credentialed mental health professional. You wouldn't let an infection fester on your body—why let one fester in your mind? Get your Best Self out there, by get the coaching if you need to do so.

Spiritual Bypass: Feel it to Heal It

As a spiritually inclined person, you may feel you should "rise above it" and have no anger about romantic relationships that didn't turn out as you'd hoped or dreamed. Just be careful not to bypass the feelings and the emotional pain. You've got to "feel it to heal it," as the saying goes. Once you've had your crying fits (dozens if you need to) and moments of fantasizing about a slow and painful death for your ex-lover, you're ready for the next step: releasing the energy that's keeping you "stuck" and resonating the "I'll never be hurt like that again" pattern.

Facing your feelings is the only way to do this. Spiritually inclined people often don't want to face their inner rage. But if it's in there, it's hurting you. Depression is sometimes called "anger turned inward" so if you're chronically sad, you may find it helpful to journal about your feelings. Write a letter to your former lover as an exercise in getting connected to your unconscious feelings about the relationship. Please don't send the letter: It's not for them, it's for you. I also suggest you avoid e-mails. It's too tempting to just hit that send button. Writing a letter out, longhand, seems to work best for most people.

Remember there's no need to send the letter. Higher self to higher self, Inner Soulmate to Inner Soulmate, your former lover "gets" what you need to say. On a soul level it's already being dealt with, but you can energize this process by reading the letter out loud. Then burn it or shred it or flush it down the toilet. You'll feel much better. (And as an added bonus there are no messy repercussions if a new lover finds it and reads it).

When Love Hurts

Although love may hurt emotionally, it never should hurt physically. If it does, you need to examine the lesson in this situation for you, and to plan a way to safely move on as soon as you can. If there is any level of physical abuse or physical pain inflicted upon you in a relationship, whether it's with a family member, a spouse, or a love interest, please seek assistance. Even if it's a once-in-a-while shove or an occasional slap, it's physical abuse. It's domestic violence. Does that seem to be a loving behavior to you? Is the person inflicting such violence, even if it's you at times or in retaliation, operating from the highest possible level, the spiritual level, their Best Self? You aren't trapped. You can leave. But do it safely: Plan, reach out for help and support; and please do it now. You'll find a list of helpful resources on page 214.

The Ache of the End

When love ends, whether the breakup is with a lover or involves the distancing of a difficult family member or friend, the heart-wrenching pain of letting go of what may once have been a treasured, thriving relationship is real. Few would argue that pain is desirable, but many would agree that the experience of *conquering* pain, of learning and growing through difficult and challenging times, is worthy and, yes, even desirable. If you've ever known someone who made it through a difficult medical situation, or who lost a loved one to death, who later said, "I learned so much about myself, I am actually grateful now for that experience," you've seen how powerful and profound a teacher pain can be.

Pain also is a reminder of how very human and sensitive you are. In some ways, although nobody wants to hear it on the heels of a breakup, pain is your gift. Pain reminds you of what deep capacity you have for love, for extending yourself, for taking a risk. Honoring your pain, allowing yourself to really experience it, is the most effective way to deal with it.

That's called vulnerability, and it's a hard lesson for many people. The connection between pain and vulnerability is inescapable. By denying pain, by pretending something doesn't hurt when it does, people are pretending to be strong when, actually, they could use some support. They prefer to look invulnerable to the outside world. They build a hard shell that is very difficult for others to crack.

Perhaps you've known someone others refer to as a softy underneath, when to the world they more closely resemble a grizzly bear then a teddy bear. That's the hard-shell-to-the-world coping style. All those grizzly bears you know are actually sensitive souls trying to find a way to avoid being hurt. Show them some compassion, and you might be surprised at how quickly their softer side is expressed.

Why Is It So Hard?

Your soul has one intention, your ego another. Your soul says, "Wow, here comes an adventure, a chance to learn, yay!" And your human ego says, "Uh oh, here comes an adventure, a chance to be hurt." Both your human ego and your soul are correct: An adventure could hurt you, but you'll also learn something.

The question, then, is: Which are you going to allow to guide to life, your soul or your ego? If you're interested in attracting soulmates into your life, one or more of whom could evolve into a Heartmate bond for the long term, you'll achieve better results by listening to your Inner Wisdom. Conquering the ego isn't an easy task, but you can learn to honor it, respect it for its desire to help you.

Then thank it and reassure it, knowing that your Inner Wisdom, your soul level of awareness, understands what the ego needs, too.

Think of your ego as a young child in need of your tender loving care and reassurance, and your soul as a compassionate, wise elder. The child within can run you if you let her, but would that be the best way to live your life? Listening to a 4-year-old's view on how to do things? Probably not. Letting your inner 4-year-old out to play now and then is a great idea, but letting her make important decisions about your life, conscious or unconscious, isn't the best plan.

Being clear and conscious, self-aware—you might even say soul-aware—helps you live more fully, more authentically. Authenticity brings many more opportunities for soulmate relationships (romantic or otherwise). But to get to that deeply authentic place, you'll need to pay ongoing attention to whether your inner child or your Inner Wisdom has the upper hand in your life.

Are You Standing in Your Own Way?

Here is a self-assessment you can use to decide if you're broadcasting the "I won't be hurt like that again" Resonance pattern and allowing it to block your success in attracting a Heartmate.

Resonance Self-Assessment:

The "I won't be hurt like that again" Resonance Pattern

1. I tend to like drama in my life; it keeps it interesting. 1 2 3 4 5

2. You really can't trust people, particularly lovers. 1 2 3 4 5

3. When I sense someone is lying to me, I have a strong urge to investigate to find out the truth. 1 2 3 4 5

4. I am perfectly happy without a satisfying romance; my life is full in other ways. 1 2 3 4 5

5. I generally see the world from the glass half-empty-perspective; I'm a bit negative about how I see the future. 1 2 3 4 5

6. I have been known to break up with someone just so they wouldn't break up with me; it hurts less that way. 1 2 3 4 5

7. I've been told that I push people away by being aggressive and challenging. 1 2 3 4 5

8. I feel safer by myself. 1 2 3 4 5

Total: "I won't be hurt like that again" pattern:_____

Score:	Interpretation:
32 to 40	You have strong elements of this Resonance Pattern on a regular basis; it's a major block for you to clear.
24 to 31	You show aspects of this pattern; it's a potential block to which you should pay attention.
15 to 23	This is an occasional Resonance Pattern for you.
14 or less	This Resonance Pattern isn't a block for you.

Attracting the ideal Heartmate requires trust in your Inner Wisdom and a willingness to be vulnerable. You can't be vulnerable if you're hiding behind the "I won't be hurt like that again" shield. And because you can't be hurt in exactly the same way, you don't need the shield anymore. It's absolute truth that you won't be hurt like that again. You can't be. It's different Now. You're different Now.

So you may as well put down the shield and join the Heartmate adventure.

Chapter 16:
All The Good Ones Are Gone

Believe that life is worth living, and your belief will help create the fact.

—*William James*

Many people give up on ever finding a special someone, a true Heartmate, a romantic soulmate with whom they could enjoy loving companionship. They give up because they mistakenly believe that "all the good ones are gone." Don't fall into the trap that this belief represents. If you feel—even just a tiny bit—that the *real* soulmates you could be happy with aren't available because they're in other relationships, or married, you're broadcasting "all the good ones are gone." That Personal Resonance blocks opportunities for Heartmate relationships. And if you're seeking a romantic soulmate, opportunity is your best friend.

Plus the idea that all the good ones are gone is simply ludicrous. You're living proof. You're a good one and you are available for better opportunities, whether with new Heartmates, Karmic Connections and Balance Partners, or even within your existing romantic relationship. And because the working definition of a soulmate is very simple one (*a soulmate is someone with whom you have an affinity, a connection),* you've got plenty of opportunities to find a good one—or several.

To follow your Inner Wisdom to a soulmate who can evolve into a Heartmate, a truly deep romantic love, you must broaden your perspective. Perhaps even redefine what a "good one" is. You must be willing to recognize that at age 30 or 40 or 50, people have histories you will need to accommodate. Flexibility is required to adapt to complications such as ex-spouses and children. Much of your success in attracting a Heartmate will depend on how fluid and flexible you can be with material-world realities. If you really can't abide the thought of someone else's children in your life, your definition of a "good one" is narrowed. You'll still have opportunities, just different ones, and maybe fewer of them.

The bottom line is this: The good ones aren't gone. They might be overlooked or misunderstood, or laying low while they put the needs of their children first for a time, or in the midst of life changes, or pulled in several different directions (just as you are). But there are still plenty of them out there. Just start focusing with an open-minded, open-hearted awareness and a clear intention that you're ready for a Heartmate bond, and you'll soon see good ones everywhere.

I'm not recommending that you settle either. You should aim high on that soul-development ranking. You should absolutely send out a Personal Resonance that is powerful, positive, and values-based. By focusing on qualities of the soul, not dollars in the wallet, degrees on the wall, or hairs on the head, you will soon discover the Universe abounds with compatible people. Remember that attachments limit you. In a Heartmate search, if you're serious, you must be open to exploring opportunities that your Inner Wisdom places before you. Those are not always likely to be exactly what you imagined. Your Inner Wisdom may test you a bit, to see if you're really sincere. Could you become interested in someone who doesn't meet your "standards" on a material level? Could you love a preschool teacher as easily as you could love a vice president of a big corporation?

As you learn to access and listen to your Inner Wisdom, you may discover that you've been walling yourself off from opportunities to find true Heartmates through your belief in scarcity, that there simply aren't enough good potential partners out there. That "all the good ones are gone" viewpoint, whether it's conscious or not, has been blocking your progress.

Even when you're joking with friends as you trade dating war stories over a few margaritas, saying, "All the good ones are gone" (even in jest), programs that thought into your Personal Resonance.

Your intentions, your thoughts, drive your life. Your Personal Resonance is a higher order form of the Law of Attraction. You really *do* manifest in your life what you believe to be true. That self-talk matters. If you believe in scarcity, whether it's with potential Heartmates or some other area of your life, the Universe will respond to you and prove to you that *you're* right. But wouldn't you rather be happy than right?

Back to Balance

If you're out of balance on the soul level you'll see that imbalance reflected somewhere in your life, often in your relationships. Relax, you're not alone: Everyone else is out of balance to some degree, too. That's what makes us human. That's what makes all relationships, even soulmate relationships, challenging at times. Even so, human life is about learning to honor your Inner Wisdom; accept your divine spiritual nature and act from it with intention. It's about learning to be "divinical," as my students jokingly term it. It's about being your Best Self.

Establishing a standard of excellence *that you can also meet* is the way to attract people who are at your level of personal development. Be realistic. Don't decide that, as a minimum-wage worker and part-time student, you'll only accept a heart surgeon for your next romantic relationship. Or that because you have a master's degree, anyone with Heartmate potential must also. Don't limit your possibilities. Instead be ready to welcome another person who, as you do, strives to do better, to be better. To advance from where they are right Now. Then make the journey to your Best Selves together, side by side, as Balance Partners and romantic Heartmates.

As you know, what you put out there, you pull toward you. Excellence attracts excellence. Ambition attracts ambition. So, before you start becoming exceedingly picky, take a thorough look at your own self on all levels: spiritual, emotional, intellectual, and physical. Are you actively expressing yourself in those four key areas? Maybe you're great with physical, tending well to your health and well being, but you haven't read a fiction book in years or taken a class just for fun. Again, it's balance that matters.

Next!

Maybe you're doing fine in all areas of life but still not attracting that Heartmate relationship. That may be because you're not resonating that "new possibilities welcomed joyfully" vibe. If you've been tossing aside potential suitors for such perceived infractions as being shorter or the same height as you are, or not earning enough, or for some other perceived shortcoming based on standards of the material world, you've been using the "all the good ones are gone" block, consciously or not. You've decided arbitrarily that the people your Personal Resonance attracted are not good enough for you.

Be careful not to judge. There's a reason these people arrived in your life. Take your time in discerning the answers to the "why this, why now" question. Keep in mind that it's not fair to judge someone on inherited genetic traits, either. Those are not factors within their control. But what they, and you, do with that genetic inheritance is.

And be aware that sitting at home, waiting for a Heartmate to find you, is the most ineffective way to attract someone. If you're zoning out in front of the television or computer games, yakking on your cell phone about trivial issues, just passing the time online perusing dating Websites, you're resonating a vibe that basically says, "I'm not too terribly interested in what life has to offer." And you'll attract that same low-energy-low-involvement-in-life-just-hangin'-out-waiting-for-it-to-be-over vibe to you. You can't attract what you won't project.

Accentuate the Positive

Sometimes your self-talk is negative and that contributes to the "all the good ones are gone" block by adding "not that they'd be interested in me, anyway." The next time you catch yourself thinking negatively, substitute a positive thought. Program your consciousness, your Personal Resonance. Even negative traits and experiences can be given a positive spin.

Also, pay attention to what you lead with when you meet new people, whether it's online or in person. Consider what kind of Personal Resonance impression you want to make. If someone says, "Tell me about yourself," don't launch right in with, "I've been divorced twice and engaged three other times," unless you want to attract someone else who lives in the past. Focus on Now. Who are you Now? "I'm a generally happy person who tends to get a little cranky before I've had my morning coffee," which tells much more about you, with humor and a willingness to admit you're not perfect. (Imagine that.)

Learn to be in the moment Now and accentuate the positive. View your divorce or breakup as an important lesson learned with someone you once cared for deeply. I know, I know: This is your ex you're dealing with here. But it is important, and not just for your children (if you have any), to strive for a more positive perspective. It's important for you to become more positive, if that's what you want to attract in a Heartmate.

Remember: There's value in that former relationship for *you*. You invested months or years of *your* life in it. You traded *your* time for that marriage or relationship. So it must have some value. Honor yourself by accepting that. Learn to take a balanced view. Accentuate the positive at least as much as the negative. Balance your views.

Strive also for what's been called an attitude of gratitude. Keep in mind that what happened in that most recent troublesome relationship, and every other one you've been in, has shaped who you are Now, at this very moment. If you're a better person today, and you probably are because you're interested in personal growth and development, you have your ex-partners to thank on some level. Maybe it's the "I refuse to behave the way he did" reaction, but it's a good *result*. You're trying to resonate your Best Self.

What if you're still really angry at your ex? That's fine. Work with those feelings, acknowledge them, treat them gently, and release them with love. Until you can say something such as, "My ex-husband and I came together at an important time in our lives, and ended it at another key turning point. I learned from that marriage, and I wish him all the best," you're not ready to date seriously. You may find it helpful to rehearse similar statement so that when you meet someone new, you can say it comfortably without gritted teeth. The more you say it, aloud or in your mind, the more you build a positive Personal Resonance around that past relationship.

If you're tempted to tell The Entire Story in the first few months of a new relationship, resist. I repeat: Resist. Listening to someone else's tale of woe when you barely know them, whether it's a casual acquaintance from work or a new love interest, usually makes you feel uncomfortable. You want to pull back, to avoid that feeling of uninvited, forced emotional intimacy. You feel dumped on when you didn't consent to being a de facto counselor. Your tale of woe will likely have the same impact on someone else. Save it for your therapist.

You may be thinking, "What? I shouldn't talk about how horrible my ex was for at least a few months into a new relationship?" Not only that, I recommend that you not talk about how horrible your ex was at all. Ever. Instead, focus on what you learned. The good points about someone you once loved. Resonating self-empowerment, self-awareness, and compassion for others attracts a better class of potential Heartmates, people who also are self aware and compassionate.

And really, is there any need for big drama? "Oh, the woman he left me for? She's 12 years younger than me. She worked with him, and she was also married. Now they think they're soulmates...." You can practically feel the eye-rolling response to having to listen to someone's diatribe about a former love interest.

The less dramatic—but still true—version of the story is, "He cheated so I ended the relationship." Done. Keep it short. Later, when you're feeling a stronger emotional bond, you may decide to share more detail. But offering too much information—and especially too much information too soon—is probably the number-one reason fledgling romantic soulmate relationships don't evolve.

Be a Good One to Attract a Good One

Your Personal Resonance broadcasts a message, and part of that Personal Resonance is your personal style. If it walks like a duck, and talks like a duck, people will assume it's a duck. People make snap judgments. They think nerdy clothes equal nerdy guy, trashy clothes equal trashy woman, fashionable clothes equal possibly gay guy or shallow woman. Even if it's untrue, people will attribute a great deal to you just based on your clothing. About 80 percent of what people process comes visually, so take the time to make a good visual impression.

Before you defiantly don that ratty sweatshirt or those beat-up jeans, declaring that any person worth having will see your inner beauty and spiritual nature underneath that scruffy exterior, it's time to rethink your plan. What kind of visual impression are you giving off? That you're a slob and just don't care? That you want someone to see your intrinsic worth, but you're going to make them work to notice you in the first place? Maybe that fashion defiance is just a way of keeping potential Heartmate relationships at a safe distance.

You endeavor to show your Best Self in other high-stakes situations, such job interviews. Don't you think attracting your potential life partner, your Heartmate, is a pretty high stakes situation? Your personal style transmits important information. Make sure it's what you want to transmit. (Suffice it to say the woman in a long white lace dress at a friend's wedding didn't present herself as wanting to celebrate the union.) If your personal style still reflects the 80s, is overly sexually suggestive, or just appears to be completely random, it's time to reprogram your appearance along with your Personal Resonance.

Form and Function

It's hard to like, let alone love, your body particularly in a culture that scrutinizes and magnifies every perceived flaw. Everyone struggles with it. My hands are far from small and delicate, and I can't grow long, elegant nails. But every day I thank them for what they help me to do. They are magnificent. I've learned to appreciate function when I can't appreciate form. So give yourself a break. Be grateful. Appreciate your body for what it does for you. Treat it kindly, with respect.

If you can't say, "I'm beautiful"—that's a tough one for most people—say, "I'm magnificent." Because it's true: You are a marvel, a unique soul in an equally unique body that does amazing things (wink, wink). Once you program that into your Personal Resonance, you'll find there are plenty of potential Heartmates out there.

And just as you are, most of them aren't age 23 and at the peak of their physical attractiveness. But magnificent, absolutely.

Just as you are.

Where It Comes From

The "All the good ones are gone" Resonance Pattern is based on scarcity thinking. If you believe in all or nothing, that there can't possibly be enough of (name something) for everyone who wants that something, you may be using this block unconsciously. In addition, people who judge on aesthetics and appearances, or who have a strong materialistic inclination, often have this block.

If you've ever decided someone was too short, too tall, or too anything else before giving him an opportunity, if you sat through the entire first date thinking, "He's 5 feet 6 inches and I'm 5 feet 7 inches so it'll never work" or, "She's not as thin as my last girlfriend" you're comparing and judging. That works against a positive, powerful, inviting Personal Resonance that attracts many more potential soulmates so you can develop a true Heartmate bond. Learn to set aside judgment and enjoy the Now with each person you meet.

Adopt an "I'm curious" attitude. It's a great way to avoid asking a direct question, too. Feeling that you're being interrogated is always unnerving, and dating is anxiety inducing already. So put people at ease with how you elicit information from them. Instead of asking, "Why do you raise peacocks?" say, "I'm curious about your peacocks." Don't go overboard: "I'm fascinated" doesn't work nearly as well as simply being curious.

When you can see that *everyone* is a good one, even if not for you, your world will change because you'll have opened your heart. You'll see that there's an innate goodness, a divine spark deep down inside. You'll see, and encourage, that little light, that shining soul resonance, that inner beauty in everyone you meet. Maybe it's hidden by 20 extra pounds, a bad haircut, or unfashionable clothes, but it's there. When you look for that first, and present yourself as curious to learn more, you'll attract that Heartmate. You may even have to choose from several good possibilities.

Here's a self-assessment you can take to help you discover whether you have the "all the good ones are gone" block in your Personal Resonance.

Resonance Self-Assessment:

The "All the good ones are gone" Resonance Pattern

1. I think that I can't compete with other people when it comes to attracting romantic partners. 1 2 3 4 5

2. Most of my friends are married or partnered, and I think about that often, wondering when it'll be my turn. 1 2 3 4 5

3. I notice details of appearance and sometimes can't get past certain things about potential romantic partners. 1 2 3 4 5

4. At times I've given up on dating because I feel there's no point to it because the kind of people I'm interested in tend to be married or involved. 1 2 3 4 5

5. I would have a hard time dating someone who doesn't match what I consider to be "my type." 1 2 3 4 5

6. I would have a hard time dating someone who's not of the same race, class, and/or educational level as me. 1 2 3 4 5

7. I'm not usually considered a risk-taker in life; I've tended to play it safe in most areas, romance included. 1 2 3 4 5

8. I would have a hard time introducing someone who's not "what they expect" to my family and friends because I worry about what they'd think. 1 2 3 4 5

Total: "All the good ones are gone" resonance pattern:_____

Score:	Interpretation:
32 to 40	You have strong elements of this Resonance Pattern on a regular basis; it's a major block for you to clear.
24 to 31	You show aspects of this pattern; it's a potential block to which you should pay attention.
15 to 23	This is an occasional Resonance Pattern for you.
14 or less	This Resonance Pattern isn't a block for you.

If you've taken the "All the good ones are gone" statement to heart in the past, Now is the time to open your heart and release that limiting view. Replace it with a statement such as this: "Abundance is mine, and I am grateful." Abundance is all around you, on all levels, and it includes soulmates of all kinds. Yes, even Heartmates, if you learn to see it that way.

And that's your choice to make.

Chapter 17:
The Five Big Lessons

Healing does not come from anyone else. You must accept guidance from within.

—From *A Course in Miracles, (Text, p. 134)*

Soulmate relationships of all types, Karmic Connections, Balance Partners, and Heartmates, are the playing ground where soul-level learning occurs. What I term the Five Big Lessons are the main overarching themes of the soul-level lessons I've seen people struggling with as I've assisted them as an intuitive consultant. Just about any problem between people can be identified as stemming from one of these five broad areas, whether it's a family conflict, a workplace tension, or a challenge within a romantic relationship.

Each of following five chapters will delve into one of these Five Big Lessons in greater detail, providing opportunities for you to consider as you ponder, journal easily in reach, what the primary Big Lesson you're dealing with in a particular relationship is. Be sure to jot down impressions, insights, reflections, questions, and memories that arise as you read though these chapters of *Natural-Born Soulmates*.

Invite your Inner Wisdom to provide guidance and insight so you can be as spiritually efficient as possible as you move toward improving your relationship life through greater understanding and awareness. Here's a brief introduction to each of the Five Big Lessons to get you thinking.

1. The Lesson of Passion

Whether it's zest for life or sexual passion for a lover, one of the Five Big Lessons you are meant to deal with on a soul level is passion. If you're not sure what your passion is, or how to reinvigorate that excitement for life (or a person you love), you'll find the Lesson of Passion reflected in at least one area, and usually several areas, of your life. You'll see opportunities to rediscover and live from your passion among soulmates of all types: Karmic Connections, Balance Partners, and Heartmates.

2. The Lesson of Purpose

Some people seem born with a sense of purpose. They know precisely what their mission is in life. But for most people, the Lesson of Purpose is an evolution. Finding your purpose on a soul level is an ongoing life lesson because it evolves and changes as you evolve and change. But there's always a key theme, a golden thread that shines throughout the tapestry of your life. The Lesson of Purpose is to discover that golden thread. Your soulmates are pieces to the puzzle of the Lesson of Purpose. Pay attention to the lessons they bring and you'll find your purpose much more easily.

3. The Lesson of Potential

Living as fully and as joyfully as possible, thriving, is what the Lesson of Potential is all about. The gifts and talents you brought with you into this world from the moment you were born are meant to be shared with the world, and the people in it. The Lesson of Potential is all about sorting out how to live so that all the seeds planted in you have the opportunity to take root and flower. Your Karmic Connections, Balance Partners, and Heartmates are all part of your Lesson of Potential.

4. The Lesson of Pacing

In this earthly world, time is a construct that must be dealt with. It's not part of the realm of the soul, which is timeless, infinite, and eternal. The only place to learn the Lesson of Pacing—you might also think of it as patience—is right here. And it's learned through the challenges and the triumphs of life with soulmates. Those unavoidable lessons in human form are what make the journey here worth taking. If you're stuck in lessons around timing—you're ready to commit and the other person isn't, for example—you can be sure your soul-level learning is about the Lesson of Pacing.

5. The Lesson of Problem-Solving

As is the case with the Lesson of Pacing, this soul-level lesson also is firmly rooted in the earthly world. Here on earth, anyone at any time can decide to make choices that directly affect the lives and therefore the choices of others. The human exercise of free will creates problems. But it can also solve them. The Lesson of Problem-Solving is about collaborating with your soulmates to address and resolve the problems created by that greatest of treasures and biggest of lessons: human free will. Sometimes you're with particular soulmates to help focus on a common problem, working as a sort of project team.

The structured framework I've developed in this book of three types of soulmates, five types of blocks to Heartmate attraction, and the Five Big Lessons is meant to provide you a structure within which to explore your own Knowing, your own Inner Wisdom. But you may find that other ideas and insights present themselves for your consideration. Consider those *aha!* moments as little reminder messages from your Inner Wisdom. So as you read and react to the ideas and concepts in the next several chapters, be sure to let that still small voice of your soul, ever prompting you to the highest levels of spiritual achievement, be heard.

And let it be honored. Just as I do, your Inner Wisdom wants to help you get the most out of your life on every possible level.

Chapter 18:
The Lesson of Passion

The greatest gift we can give one another is rapt attention to one another's existence.

—Sue Atchley Ebaugh

When you are passionate about something, whether it's an activity or a person, challenges seem rare. And your passion helps you overcome the ones you do face. Whether it's passion for your career, passion for a leisure activity, or passion for your beloved, and the Lesson of Passion on the soul level is all about staying engaged, keeping connected, feeling excitement.

Why then do so many soulmate relationships that appear to have passion, particularly sexual passion, fail? Usually the misplacement or misunderstanding of Lesson of Passion is the root of the problem. Karmic Connections, those lower-level, blast-from-the-past, unfinished-business soulmates, are often involved in relationships where Lesson of Passion is a focal point. The unfinished business that brought you two together this time around is often wrapped in urgency, in passion.

Once you've handled the unfinished business, you may find that your level of passion dissipates. The fire goes out of the relationship because there's nothing that feels as if it's urgent. Your business together is finished. At that point you must redefine what passion means to you, and discern whether you've mistaken a sexual passion or infatuation for emotional passion, true love. That's often a tough discernment to make because often the unfinished business with a Karmic Connection is related to a romantic involvement from a past life that didn't end well. Anyone who's had a passionate sexual encounter after a huge fight knows how closely emotional and physical passion are linked and how difficult it is to sort out Karmic Connections from true Heartmate bonds.

All fires burn to embers if untended. If you're both willing to tend the fire of passion by continuing to fuel it, Karmic Connection relationships can shift relatively smoothly into Balance Partner and eventually true Heartmate status. There's no guarantee of success of course because that pesky free-will business is involved. You both must agree to work on moving the relationship along.

Adrenaline Junkies

You may especially like the adrenaline rush that accompanies romantic passion. You may find you can't maintain interest in someone after you've begun a sexual relationship because the chase is where you find the highest levels of adrenaline. If you're what I call a passion junkie, the drama attracts your attention and keeps that feeling of aliveness and vibrancy going. That drama keeps your adrenaline engaged. Think of a roller coaster ride and compare it to a nice gentle canoe ride across a quiet lake. Both have their value.

As most people do, you might enjoy a brief ride on a roller coaster for the excitement of the endorphin and adrenaline rush. But if you're one of those people who require constantly high levels of passion in your relationships, examine whether you are mistaking adrenaline-rush excitement for real passion for the other person. Is it an adrenaline and endorphin rush, or true Heartmate love?

A steady, quiet passion that perseveres also has its place. Embers can be reignited, too. Remember Edison? It was patience and passion for his quest that allowed him to say invested in his dream to create the light bulb. He must have had *aha!* moments of passion that reengaged him in his task and kept him moving forward.

Striking a balance is key. Remember the infinity symbol? It only can go on forever because it's in balance. The outward flow and the inward flow are in equal proportion. The yin (inward chi) and yang (outward chi) flow smoothly.

The Lesson of Passion and Karmic Connections

Because it's the lesson that's important to your soul, not necessarily the person or the relationship in which you learn it, you may find a lesson (person) in the workplace today that was a lesson (person) from a marriage in a past life. Perhaps in that previous life you shared, the Lesson of Passion centered on sexual passion. Currently, the Lesson of the Passion with that very same soulmate, who is now in your life as a workplace colleague, shifts arenas. Today, the Lesson of Passion is part of a shared vision within the workplace. A desire to achieve great things with a product or service as business partners, for example, is the Lesson of Passion played out at work. (And maybe this is why people often say that being in business together is similar being married.)

You can see how easily a remembrance from a past life of unfinished business dealing with sexual passion could become misinterpreted in this current life experience with your Karmic Connection, who's now a business colleague. In such a situation, the Lesson of Passion is about broadening your perspective and expressing your passion on a different level, in different way. The lesson is that passion is not always of a sexual nature. Of course, unless you and your Karmic Soulmate have completely resolved and learned the soul-level lesson of appropriate sexual passion, the two of you are at risk to misinterpret the Lesson of Passion. You could end up, for example, having an illicit workplace affair that leads to even more complications—and more messy karma to deal with one day.

In terms of the seven basic chakras, or energy centers, sexual passion is a lesson first addressed in the lower chakras. As you move through lifetime after lifetime, you learn to reinterpret passion in the context of those higher-level chakras. You must move through the lessons of emotional passion and into the higher realms of intellectual and spiritual passions. A solid and well-balanced understanding of sexual passion puts in place a beautiful foundation for other kinds of passion, and the best kind of all: a passion that connects on all levels—physically, emotionally, intellectually, and spiritually.

Here are a few suggestions on how you can bring clarity to the Lesson of Passion with blast-from-the-past Karmic Soulmates.

Exercise One: Ask Your Inner Soulmate

If you find yourself having sexual fantasies about someone you really have no current interest in as a potential Heartmate (a "no-strings" kind of connection), or are the target of sexual interest you don't return, realize that it may be residual energy from a previous experience with that person, a past-life encounter. While in meditation, mentally ask your Inner Soulmate for insights about the attraction. Relax and let yourself drift back to previous experiences with the person you are now challenged by. Ask questions such as, "When did we know each other? Under what circumstances did we know each other? Where were we known to each other? What was left unfinished?" Allow images, symbols, and other information brought to you through the guidance of your Inner Soulmate arise. Intend that you will easily recall this information when your period of reflection and meditation is complete. Use your journal to record this information and save it for later review.

Exercise Two: Be Here Now

Bring your consciousness to the moment, Now. See you and your Karmic Soulmate as you are known to each other today. Send as much healing love as you can imagine, the unconditional kind devoid of sexual overtones, to the two of you. Allow this love to take the form of a beautiful iridescent bubble that encompasses you both. Then, use your Personal Resonance to program a different current experience with this Karmic Connection soulmate. Mentally state your intentions and boundaries for the relationship. For example, you might intend something along the lines of, "We are passionate in our work together, but feel no sexual passion toward each other." This technique can be used also as a writing exercise if you prefer. Simply write out, by hand, your intentions for this Karmic Connection, and how you'd like to see it evolve.

Remember: Only Now has power. By using the present moment Now to address a previous experience with a Karmic Connection soulmate (data now stored in that soul-level database that you are building as you grow and evolve), you're being responsible and spiritually efficient. Being clear and precise about what you want in those relationships is often the most difficult aspect when it comes to the Lesson of Passion. The residual soul-level memories of a sexually passionate love affair between you and someone you now know as a Karmic Connection can be used to either rekindle that sexual passion, or to spur a different kind of passion: an emotional or intellectual passion.

What you program into your Personal Resonance, and how your Karmic Connection soulmate reacts to that intentional and focused use of your free will, determines the outcome. As you seek clarity and insight about how to best learn the Lesson of Passion in the moment Now, with this particular Karmic Connection soulmate, remember to always approach the situation as a learning experience from which you will both gain. That intention alone will clear up quite a bit of unfinished business and keep the passion in its place—wherever you decide that place may be.

The Lesson of Passion and Balance Partners

If you are working on the Lesson of Passion with a Balance Partner, you're not as likely to feel the tug of sexual interest. The reason is that you are already in balance when it comes to the Lesson of Passion, at least on the lower chakra levels. You have now moved into higher order expressions of the Lesson of Passion. With a Balance Partner soulmate, you are likely to feel that wonderful sense of shared vision—excitement about an issue or a goal. You're engaged emotionally and intellectually first.

Perhaps you've experienced the almost telepathic understanding of shared passion that Balance Partners often have when on a sports team or in a creative or intellectual pursuit shared with others, such as at school or work. If you think back to your childhood, to a friend with whom you clicked easily and comfortably, and with whom you shared a passion for soccer or music or art or some other interest, you'll understand the experience of the Lesson of Passion that has no sexual overtones. It's a beautiful feeling to be with people who seem to "get you" from a soul level.

Generally, when the Lesson of Passion with Balance Partners dates back to childhood, it's experienced with people of roughly the same age and gender. In adulthood, many people experience the Lesson of Passion with Balance Partners in a more intellectual way, sharing a common interest in developing a skill. You might find Balance Partner soulmates applying the intellectual version of Lesson of Passion in a community group or adult school class.

Balance Partners are the soulmates you've already built a nice foundation with, and they offer wonderful opportunities to evolve into Heartmates. You might discover a romantic interest in each other, a sexual passion, grows the more you share your emotional and intellectual passions.

What if You Don't Feel That Chemistry?

If you are looking to build or rekindle passion with an existing Balance Partner you see as a potential Heartmate, understand that the roller-coaster ride feeling of infatuation may not be there at the outset. That's probably a good thing, as the roller-coaster experiences tend to be with lower-level (in terms of the chakras) soulmates. Through time you develop that persistent, gentle flame that is a sort of pilot light, a flame that can be switched to high at any time.

The trouble is that people often mistake that roller-coaster feeling of falling in love for true all-levels-engaged passion. Generally, it's not. It's sexual chemistry, lower chakra-focused energy. If you are attracted to someone you feel strong infatuation or even obsession for, be ready: It's Karmic Connection time; there's cleanup work to do. Be warned: This isn't going to be an easy journey.

Keep in mind that Karmic Connection soulmates are the lowest on the totem pole of soulmate relationships. They roughly represent the lower chakras, the physical realms. These are the situations in which the past-life energies and lessons must be integrated. Such lessons may include violence, betrayal, murder, and mayhem. Because we grow and evolve in the spirit world, thankfully we don't have to repeat the same mistakes. Instead, as we move into Balance Partner status we get to make other ones. What an efficient system! There are more chances to make mistakes, but those are just more opportunities for your soul to grow.

Exactly how you resolve issues with your soulmates largely depends on your current soulmate relationship: Karmic Connection, Balance Partner, or Heartmate. These categories ebb and flow, shift around and change based on many factors. The most important factor is, of course, your Personal Resonance, that soul essence that makes you unique and special.

Take a few moments to think over with who in your life you have worked on the Lesson of Passion. In which situations has it been messy? Difficult? Painful? Those are your Karmic Connection levels. In which situations have you felt supported and comfortable, sharing an excitement together that stands apart from sexuality? Those are your Balance Partners. Finally, think about with whom in your life you have learned the Lesson of Passion from the status of Heartmate, a place where you felt connected and engaged on all levels: spiritually, intellectually, emotionally, and physically.

If you haven't experienced that kind of engaged-on-all-levels relationship yet, you can. Clarity, intention, and free will can take you there. Get a very clear idea in your mind of what that experience would be like for you. Use the Power of Now to create a sense of bonding, of passion—spiritual, intellectual, emotional, and sexual.

Do it Now, using the power of your Personal Resonance. Make it big. Make it real. Send that powerful vision out to the farthest reaches of the Universe. Next, delegate your Inner Soulmate to be responsible for bringing you Heartmate relationship candidates, ones with whom you already have grown through the Balance Partner stage. By working with your Inner Wisdom, your Inner Soulmate, you can learn all about the Lesson of Passion on all levels, which is much more spiritually efficient. You learn on the levels of body, mind, and spirit, on the levels of physical, emotional, intellectual, and spiritual, simultaneously.

So, transmit your desire to learn as much as possible in a truly powerful Heartmate bond. Broadcast that vibration, that unique Personal Resonance, that beautiful soul essence. Then, get ready to reap a harvest of intriguing new soulmates, including your next Heartmate.

Chapter 19:
The Lesson of Purpose

If you're able to be yourself, then you have no competition. All you have to do is get closer and closer to that essence.

—*Barbara Cook*

Understanding who you really are and how you fit into the larger Universe is what I call the Lesson of Purpose. Why are you here on earth? What gifts are here to share? What do you want to do with your life while you're here?

On a basic level, the Lesson of the Purpose is all about declaring your intentions. It's about deciding what you want while remaining devoid of attachments to any particular outcome—using your free will. It's about putting your Personal Resonance to work in the world with a conscious, deliberate focus. And, as in all the Big Lessons, the Lesson of Purpose is understood first at a basic level and later at a more layered level. It, too, begins at the lower chakra levels and moves upward to the higher levels of complexity over lifetime after lifetime.

The Lesson of Purpose and Karmic Connection Soulmates

With Karmic Connection soulmates, the Lesson of Purpose often is about separating completely from their influence so that you're able to hear your own Inner Voice, to allow yourself to be guided to your life's purpose, rather than follow a script that someone else has developed. Because of the strong influence of family members, particularly when you are young, learning the Lesson of Purpose often happens within the immediate family.

An example of a Karmic Connection and the Lesson of Purpose within a family context is someone who was discouraged in childhood from following her talents and interests and pushed toward more "practical options." The girl who wanted to be a musician but trained to become a certified public accountant may enjoy her work and her life, but her calling, her desire on a soul level, her soul's purpose, may well have been to become a musician.

The Lesson of Purpose for her is to heal any lingering resentments about being pushed by her family, and using her Now Power to transform the situation. To move closer to her purpose. One of the best ways to heal this kind of dilemma is to apply the practical, material world training in the arena of the soul's natural interests and its purpose. For example, an accountant who wanted to be a singer could develop a specialty in entertainment and business management for performers.

The Lesson of Purpose can also be about bridging choices you made under the influence of family with those your Inner Wisdom guides you toward. It's about honoring the family ties and your own soul's calling simultaneously. Many times the hardest lesson to learn is that you can't make everyone happy.

Within a marriage to a Karmic Connection soulmate, the Lesson of Purpose might involve finding a way to pursue a dreamed-of education when your spouse feels that it's more important to family finances that you work full time. In the workplace, the Lesson of Purpose with a Karmic Connection boss might center on clearly establishing your boundaries, to learn to say "no" when you consistently hit the 50-hour-a-week mark on what is supposed to be a 40-hour-a-week job. The boss "knows" you on a soul level as a compliant child and your Lesson of Purpose includes teaching your boss about your limits.

If you decide to honor your Inner Wisdom regarding your Lesson of Purpose, there's a good chance that some family members or workplace colleagues will be upset. Because of this, sometimes a bridge across conflicting interests is impossible to create, or once created, difficult to cross. You are then faced with deciding what's more important: your soul-level purpose or the opinions of others who are concerned about you.

The Lesson of Purpose and Balance Partner Soulmates

If your Lesson of Purpose is about learning to walk down the road less traveled to bring balance on a soul level into your life, you'll know it. Often you sense this desire to march to a different drummer from childhood, but still do your best to "fit in" to the world around you, adapt to your family's expectations. For example, I earned an economics degree and an MBA before honoring my true purpose in the world of intuition, which is definitely a road less traveled. But if you honor that Lesson of Purpose, at whatever age you build the strength to do so, you'll probably find you have much more company than expected. You'll discover an array of Balance Partners there to support you.

The Lesson of Purpose is sometimes one of setting the example for other soulmates through your own sense of inner peace, of soul-level balance. This might be done by taking a strong stance on behalf of others. For example, you might bring balance to a workplace by being a whistleblower or internal ombudsman.

Interestingly, taking a stand from your soul-level balance often creates what appear, at first, to be bigger imbalances around you. Learn to see this as part of the healing process. Still, this is a very difficult place to be, and it's why many people avoid listening to their Inner Wisdom, which is prompting them to initiate change through the Lesson of Purpose.

When the Lesson of Purpose is in great conflict with the desires of a family or the norms of a culture, periods of estrangement are not uncommon. Sometimes they last for years, even decades. Taking an unpopular stand often leads to disconnection and a sense of being shunned. The decision is much tougher when the stakes are high, or quite personal.

In such difficult circumstances, the soulmates involved are very likely Karmic Connections. When there's big drama involved—"If you marry him, don't ever set foot in this house again" or "If you don't join your cousins in the family business, you'll be written out of the will" or "If you tell the authorities she hits us we'll have nowhere to live"—you can bet it's karmic, unfinished business from somewhere in your past, including your past lives.

However, you may not be the one who needs to clear this up directly. You may be helping from the higher elevation of Balance Partner, through inspiration and emotional support. You may be playing the role of teacher by example in someone else's improvisation. That's your Lesson of Purpose with that individual: Help them become strong enough to take on the challenge of a difficult life task.

The Law of Purpose is easier to manage if you're working on it with other Balance Partners, people who've evolved beyond survival-chakra level tools such as intimidation, threats, and black-and-white, right-or-wrong thinking and can see the shades of gray. The Lesson of Purpose with Balance Partners in a workplace setting, for example, might be a shared vision of business success. Classic tales of people who started a business with a few college buddies and later became millionaires are good examples of the Lesson of Purpose demonstrated in a healthy way in a workplace setting.

Dealing with Balance Partners with whom you don't have unfinished karmic business doesn't mean the relationships with them will be stress-free. Sharing a common vision or goal doesn't mean that you will also agree on exactly how to accomplish that vision. That's the playing ground for the Lesson of Purpose among Balance Partners: the focus is the *how* as opposed to the *what* among Karmic Connections soulmates. The big drama of what to do is replaced by finer details of how to do it because you've already agreed on the purpose, the what. It becomes only a matter of how.

The Law of Purpose and Heartmates

Among those soulmates you consider to be possible Heartmates, the kind whom you could share a balanced-on-all-levels, all-chakras-engaged relationship with, the Lesson of Purpose is also about the *why* as well as the *what* and the *how*. With potential Heartmates or romantic soulmates, you're considering why you're drawn to be together, what values you share, what your goals for the future on a personal level are. The Lesson of Purpose with a potential Heartmate involves looking at who you are and who you'd like to become as you and your Heartmate grow together through the years.

Heartmate connections increase the complexity of the lessons to be learned through the Law of Purpose. With a Heartmate, you encompass more areas of life than is generally the case with Balance Partners. Decisions with a Heartmate will be about family, career, personal interests, friends, and community. To complicate things further, within each of these areas, you might have a slightly different Lesson of Purpose, although there's usually a common overall theme.

If you haven't yet found that Heartmate connection, you know where to start: with yourself. Access and apply the insights you glean from your Inner Wisdom. Endeavor to become your Best Self. Radiate a Personal Resonance of openness and joy. That's what attracts. Authenticity. Clarity. Joyfulness. Gratefulness. Flexibility.

In other words, living with a switched-on connection to your Inner Wisdom. If you're not quite sure how to get that switch turned on, here are two very simple (not necessary easy) steps:

Step one: Ask for guidance.

Step two: Act on it. Act from your deepest level, your soul, your Best Self, the place where your open heart radiates love to all. Especially to yourself.

Practical Ways to Learn the Lesson of Purpose

Here are some ways you can learn to access your Inner Wisdom and sort out how to best learn (or teach) the Lesson of Purpose through your relationships with your soulmates. First make a connection to your Inner Wisdom. Meditation and other techniques for calming and centering your mind help in this regard. It also helps to pay attention to the mundane world, the earthly world you inhabit. Listen to your Inner Wisdom, but use that great gift (your mind) too. Assess the situation with both your heart and your head.

Get out your journal and record your reactions, impressions, and other information that comes to mind as you review the following information on how to apply the Lesson of Purpose in your life. As you experiment with it, you may discover that your purpose shifts and changes. What you thought was your purpose in life is different from month to month, year to year, because you're always changing. Always evolving. So if you've been searching in vain for your purpose in life, and haven't yet found one, you can relax. There are probably several, depending on the situation, the characters, and the context.

When you're faced with a challenging situation involving a Karmic Connection soulmate, whether a family member, friend, workplace colleague, or a romantic partner, consider first how you'd like the energy between you to shift. If this situation between you and this particular soulmate were in perfect order, how would it look? This is the ideal time to call on your Inner Soulmate for assistance, to ask for guidance if you're stuck regarding what course to take.

Once you have a clear awareness, create and hold that intention in your mind. Purposefully and with clear intention send that image, that feeling, that vibration, that resonance you've created to transform the situation out into the Universe. Each time you catch yourself wondering if the situation can change, is changing, might change, might never change (basically whenever you're experiencing a moment of doubt) bring yourself back to the moment Now. Remember the power of your Personal Resonance in the Now, and your intention to broadcast love and healing.

Although your life purpose may seem to shift, or look different as you change careers and move through various stages and life experiences, in the end, it boils down to this very simple act of creating love, of resonating healing in the moment Now. The better you become at holding that creative and powerful space where anything is possible because it all comes from love, the more you will see transformations in your life, particularly with your most challenging soulmates.

Through time, you will see fewer messy situations and more balance. Through your persistent efforts at healing and transformation through the Lesson of Purpose, you'll discover that many Karmic Connections evolve into Balance Partners in your life. The payoff for taking the time to send love and healing to those who need it is additional support—friends and loved ones you can count on down the line. Serving others actually serves you, and even more so when you come from a place of nonattachment. Trusting in the Law of Resonance will ensure that you'll reap the benefits of kindnesses extended to Karmic Connections who challenge you, but also teach you.

As you continue to work with it, the Lesson of Purpose evolves to a greater, broader purpose. Your Personal Resonance extends beyond your personal world. That shining light of your soul becomes a beacon. When that happens, it becomes easier to maintain a vision of balance and ease within all your relationships, whether with family, friends, coworkers, or lovers. You won't need to spend as much time focusing so specifically on certain people and situations, either. By working on the Lesson of Purpose, your own Personal Resonance becomes more spiritually effective. This is the natural outgrowth of inviting your Inner Wisdom to assist you on a regular basis.

Building partnerships and working together with your Balance Partners is a very similar experience, except it's an entirely earth-based experience. It involves human nature as well as spiritual nature. Which, of course, means free will is involved. And that means anything can happen. When you involve your Inner Wisdom in the process, and encourage others to do the same, an almost exponential quality emerges.

A group of focused Balance Partners who share a common purpose, a focused intention, can really transform situations. So even if you enjoy your solitude, if you're happy spending a good deal of time working on your own pursuits, make room in your life for the Lesson of Purpose shared with others. It enhances and expands your Personal Resonance. That makes it even more powerful when you program it for a personal goal. In a way, giving your energy toward others is a very selfish act. But in this case, self means soul. You serve your soul when you serve others. And everybody wins.

Especially you.

Chapter 20:
The Lesson of Potential

We say we waste time, but that is impossible. We waste ourselves.

—*Alice Bloch*

The Lesson of Potential is all about discerning between potential unleashed and potential on hold. Potential unleashed means a person is actively pursuing personal growth and change, whether that is physically, emotionally, intellectually, or spiritually. Potential on hold means that a person is waiting for what they perceive to be a better time to explore and develop their gifts and talents. Energetically speaking, they're "on hold."

As with the other Big Lessons, the Lesson of Potential often requires several repetitions, in lifetime after lifetime, with a variety of soulmates, to fully understand. As discussed in Chapter 13, one of the most common blocks people experience when they begin to reprogram their Personal Resonance to more effectively attract soulmates and Heartmates is becoming too attached to someone's unleashed potential. They hang on in going-nowhere relationships that don't serve them on a soul level. Because everyone has a great deal of untapped potential, it's often very difficult to move on from such stagnant relationships.

Even for people who've learned to detach themselves from being hooked on someone else's potential and who've learned to operate from What Is Now, the Lesson of Potential is important. They, too, need to understand how best to achieve their potential, to transform stagnant energy into vibrant energy. In a universe of limitless possibilities (not probabilities but possibilities) this is where Inner Wisdom assists.

The Lesson of Potential and Karmic Connection Soulmates

With Karmic Connections, the Lesson of Potential is often about remaining unaffected by opinions and choices of others. For example, you might find yourself in a circumstance where you're being encouraged to take actions that just don't feel right to you. Perhaps you're being encouraged to use drugs or alcohol. Your Inner Wisdom is niggling away at you, encouraging you to use more of your innate potential, to be strong enough to not only walk away, but to encourage others in the direction of your choice. Step one is resisting; that's the Karmic Connection level of the Lesson of Potential. Step two is reaching out to others to assist them in resisting choices that do not serve them on a soul level, choices that would go against their Inner Wisdom, which in this type of situation is often called the conscience. Serving as an example to others elevates the lesson to Balance Partner soulmate status, with you in the role of balance-bringer.

Another example of the Lesson of Potential is gossiping about others. Many people engage in office gossip or the spreading of rumors about others they know, or know of. Maybe it seems to be a harmless way to pass time or create a diversion in a same-old, same-old workday or add interest to an otherwise pretty ho-hum life. But gossiping has a negative effect on many levels. The Lesson of Potential, in this case, is about resisting participation in behavior you yourself would not want to be the object of. By participating in negative behaviors, you limit your potential, as well as that of others you gossip about. It's also simply not spiritually efficient on a soul development level. Talking negatively about others (yes, even your ex) creates more Karmic Connections and loose ends that you'll need to tie up, in this life or some future adventure.

The Lesson of Potential and Balance Partner Soulmates

With people who are soulmates in your life there to support and encourage you, the Lesson of Potential has an entirely different effect.

Having people notice and encourage your talents is one example of the Lesson of Potential in its more positive expression.

Balance Partners are found among those teachers who comment on your skill with math, among coaches who nurture your talent in a sport you enjoy, among older relatives who remind you of ancestors who also had a gift for music or performance. The Lesson of Potential for you as the recipient of encouragement is to notice if those messages from people around you echo the voice of your soul, if they resonate with your Inner Wisdom. The degree to which you allow others to decide for you what's best is at the heart of the Lesson of Potential.

If the encouragement of others differs from the encouragement of your Inner Wisdom, the Lesson of Potential becomes one about free-will choice. Will you let the well-meaning advice of others define you? Or will you define yourself with the support of your Inner Wisdom? If you're fortunate to be multitalented, you have an even more difficult choice. Just because you *could* become an attorney or a dancer, for example, doesn't mean you *want* to become an attorney or a dancer, or that it would be in your best interests on a soul level. In this case, the Lesson of Potential with Balance Partner soulmates is all about turning away from your "comfort zones," talents you've already developed, and developing new skills and talents. At times you may decide it's best to reprogram your Personal Resonance to attract a new crop of Balance Partner soulmates who will help you with the task of self-development in a new area.

In your role as a Balance Partner for others, the Lesson of Potential is about offering input without insistence and encouraging others without becoming demanding. Let's say you're the parent of a child with evident talent for musical performance. Encouraging your child to develop his talent is one thing; living vicariously through him because you had once had the dream of becoming a musician but didn't is entirely another. The Lesson of Potential here is a delicate balance between encouraging your child to listen to their Inner Wisdom about what's right for them, and imposing your own dream or fantasy of who you'd like your child to be. When it comes to Balance Partner soulmates, being supportive but not intrusive is the Lesson of Potential.

Nonattachment also is important. The Lesson of Potential is about presenting your (informed) opinion, and then trusting that the person you're encouraging will listen to it, as well as to their Inner Wisdom. Letting go of your desires and attachments in such cases is difficult, but that's an important part of the Lesson of Potential.

The Lesson of Potential and Heartmates

Learning the Lesson of Potential with those who might become Heartmates requires even more awareness of the subtleties between desire and potential, among What I Want, What Might Be, and What Is Now. Letting go of manipulative tactics and instead trusting in your own ability to transform your Personal Resonance, your vibe (and through that to transform others around you), is the key.

Holding the energetic space that broadcasts, "Anything is possible, and I eagerly anticipate the highest and best expression of love between us on all levels" is the stance to aim for in your Personal Resonance with potential Heartmates. Seek to hold the energy of excitement, anticipation, delight, joy. But not expectation. Learning to live in the moment, Now makes potential a vibrant, charged energy that supports you, that launches you to higher and better opportunities for soul growth. And that's exactly what your Inner Wisdom wants to help you achieve: the most spiritually efficient soul growth and development. And of course, the most passion and excitement on all levels.

Practical Ways to Learn the Lesson of Potential

Here are some ways you can learn to embrace the Lesson of Potential. First, practice nonattachment. Learn to say, "I would like to see this situation happen, but I trust that whatever happens is exactly what needs to happen for the highest and best of all parties involved." You can also frame your goal statements with something along the lines of, "I gratefully welcome this situation, or something even better."

For example, let's say you've been interviewing for a job that you really feel is ideal for you at this time in your life. Use your Personal

Resonance to attract it, or something even better, by using your free will to "own" it. Practice what I call "make it real" exercises of visualization. Kids might say "put your wishies on it" or declare "dibs."

Imagine yourself on your first day of the job you want. Imagine yourself handing out your new business card, sending friends and family your new contact info in an e-mail, describing your good fortune to people you used to work with. Imagine capably managing the job and its various tasks. Be sure to not only visualize such events, but to feel them, hear them, smell them. Make this imagined job as real as possible using all your senses. Feel yourself moving around on the job: making a presentation, walking through the office. Imagine the audio track, too, the sounds you'd expect to hear on your targeted job: people chatting on their phones, the clacking of keyboards, the smells of coffee and microwaved lunches. You might find it helpful to create an art piece about what you're attracting. Draw or create a computer graphic or a collage. Then add, "And I gratefully welcome this or something even better into my life." Make that a regular practice.

This same technique can be applied to any aspect of your life. If your goal is to use your Personal Resonance to attract a Heartmate, create as much clarity as possible through visualization. See yourself with the object of your interest if you have someone in mind for Heartmate status. If you've not yet found a potential Heartmate, be careful not to be too specific about the person's appearance in your visualizations or artwork. You want to attract based on soul-level qualities. Put as much feeling as possible into this exercise. Work from your heart center and allow yourself to deeply feel that bond of love that you're creating. Then send your Personal Resonance, your intentions declared and outlined, out. Add "and I gratefully welcome this person or someone even better suited to me into my life."

If you're already involved with someone in a relationship you hope to enhance, you may experience many complications and challenges, particularly if you're with a Karmic Connection soulmate. You can help them learn the Lesson of Potential, too. Encourage that person's soul evolution and personal growth to become first a

Balance Partner, someone who loves and supports you in at least one area of your life. Later you might be able to move from there to truly-connected-on-all-levels Heartmate status. Start where you are and see how much your free will and your Personal Resonance can accomplish, with some nudges from your Inner Soulmate (and of course theirs).

Use the visualization and feeling-based creative exercise previously described to demonstrate on an energetic level, from your Inner Wisdom, what you'd like the relationship to be. See yourselves engaged intellectually in a discussion of current events. See yourselves engage emotionally in an activity that seems touching and romantic to you: holding hands as you walk along a beach, dancing slowly together, looking deeply into each other's eyes (the windows to the soul, remember) over the flame of a candle at a celebration dinner that marks a special occasion in your lives.

I suggest you stay away from lower-chakra-based or highly sexual imagery, however, if you want to move the relationship to higher levels of expression. You want to heal the Karmic Connections and improve the emotional balance. So, instead of sexual imagery, focus on the emotional and romantic imagery—but don't forget that lovely feeling of anticipation of what happens *after* that. Just as a movie shows only the door closing but not what's happening behind it, focus on the leading-up-to part of the interaction.

You may not be able to encourage someone with a nasty temper to join an anger-management program, or spend more time with you if work is their primary focus, but you can work from the level of *your* Personal Resonance and focus on transforming theirs. Send out that clear intention of what you want toward them as though it's a shining ray of sunlight. The more your partner is responsive to your Personal Resonance on an energetic level, the more movement and change you'll see. You'll notice that they start making long-awaited changes on their own. Be careful not to let resentment of the "why did it take so long?" type creep into your consciousness. Accept the changes gratefully, and acknowledge your part in the process of transformation.

This process definitely works, but for it to work at its best you must truly be ready, emotionally and spiritually, for that situation you programmed to evolve. Even if it means moving away from each other if that's what your Inner Wisdom presents. If you develop a daily practice of envisioning a transformed relationship and use your Personal Resonance with clear and high intentions, and you notice a distancing effect rather than the tighter emotional bond you're seeking, that's a sign that your Inner Wisdom is bringing you the "something better" that you programmed. Although it's painful to let go of the hope that someone you care about deeply will grow into the person you know that they can become, making room in your life for something that better serves *you* better on a soul level.

Gratitude and gentleness are also important elements of the Lesson of Potential. Demanding of others doesn't work. Requesting is the better way to get what you want. So request of your Inner Wisdom, don't demand. Request gentler endings and transformations. Demanding gentleness doesn't work because it's a mismatch energetically. How can you be both gentle and demanding? Your Personal Resonance carries the vibration, the tone of your desires as well as the content when you program it. You've probably said, "It's not what she said that bothered me so much as *the way that she said it*" at some point. You're reacting to the dissonance between what was said and what you felt intuitively in that individual's Personal Resonance.

Gratitude and appreciation elevate the tone of any request. They take it to a higher level. And if you're in this for the highest and best, gratitude for What Is Now as well as What Might Be only enhances your broadcast, the power of your Personal Resonance.

The Lesson of Potential comes down to this: Live up to your own potential, become your Best Self, and you'll attract soulmates who do the same. That Heartmate you're seeking can find you much more easily when you shine your brightest.

Chapter 21:
The Lesson of Pacing

No longer forward nor behind
I look in hope or fear;
But, grateful take the good I find,
The best of now and here.

—*John Greenleaf Whittier*

From the perspective of human life, timing is everything. From the perspective of the soul, timing is the *only* thing because the only place you have power is in the moment Now. And your soul lives always in the moment Now.

The Lesson of Pacing encourages you to balance the power of the moment with the fact that here, on earth, people are bound by time in their day-to-day lives. Timing is what sequences human life and allows you to focus on one thing at a time (or at least, try to). But it's also perhaps the most frustrating element of human life. You don't have the time to do everything. So get some help: Ask your Inner Wisdom what belongs at the top of your personal priority list.

The Lesson of Pacing and Karmic Connection Soulmates

Challenging relationships with lots of unfinished business often remain unresolved because of the Lesson of Pacing. With Karmic Connections, the Lesson of Pacing is about when people come into each others' lives, how long they stay, and sometimes the back-and-forth dance of leave-return-leave again.

First one leaves, deciding the pace within the relationship has been too slow. The other quickens the pace in response, so then they get back together. And they repeat this cycle yet again. Neither wants the other to "win" the race between them. The back-and-forth drama of the Lesson of Pacing is seen in all types of relationships, from runaway teens to runaway brides, and even unable-to-commit partners. Perhaps you've been locked in the Lesson of Pacing with someone and felt as if you literally were pacing the floor. Back and forth. Back and forth. Eventually, one of the two parties in any relationship must be willing to allow the pacing to shift so that they're moving in the same direction at the same speed.

Let's say you've been in a relationship for several years and are approaching what you consider the now-or-never point. You always felt you wanted to be married by age 30 with a child by 33. But your partner has a different plan. He's happy waiting an additional two or three years until he's achieved a particular level of career success. Which of you adjusts your plan? That depends on many factors, of course, but a big factor is flexibility—both yours and his. The Lesson of Pacing becomes a negotiation about the timing of events in your lives, together and separately.

What about a situation in which you've been divorced a few years and meet someone at work who's been separated, but is still legally married. He says he wants to end his marriage. He acts as if he's divorced, but he isn't. The Lesson of Pacing in this scenario is about the energetic loose ends, what I'll call "merged fields." He hasn't cleared the field with his current wife. They're still merged energetically. They are much more connected right Now than they would be if they were formally divorced. The Lesson of Pacing in such a situation concerns whether or not you're comfortable developing a relationship with someone who's technically still married. And for him, the Lesson of Pacing is about sorting out why he can't let go. He moves between the two of you, pacing back and forth.

Similarly complex situations involving people who are married or committed but who are involved in affairs but not contemplating divorce or a breakup abound. And the parties involved invariably believe they're soulmates. That they're meant to be together.

Well, it's true that they are soulmates—but most likely the messy kind: Karmic Connections. You know these relationships are emotionally messy. You've seen them among friends or at work. Perhaps you've even been in one yourself. Maybe you already know that in most affairs (about 90 percent based on some studies), the couple breaks up if either one leaves their primary relationship.

The Lesson of Pacing in such circumstances is about knowing when to say when. When to let go of the starry-eyed notion that this person who already has a primary involvement *really* has your best interests at heart. If he did, he'd either end it with you, or leave the other relationship to be with you. He'd stop pacing between you. He'd endeavor to clear up the messy energy fields, starting with his. And if subterfuge or lying is involved, clearly the goal of presenting one's Best Self isn't at the top of the list.

The Lesson of Pacing when someone is open and honest about being involved with two people and claiming to love them both often is no less painful than an illicit affair, however. The back-and-forth cycle wears on the parties involved, even the person in the middle who can't make up his or her mind. In this case, clarity in your Personal Resonance will enhance the other person's clarity because your energy fields are merged due to your involvement. Decide what you want. Clearly project that vision. If the other person's resonance and yours are aligned, if your Inner Soulmates concur that this is a relationship that works on a soul level for both of you, you'll see transformations begin. Clarity attracts clarity.

Another example of the Lesson of Pacing in action concerns how many years you have together. Let's say you have a beautiful relationship with a soulmate, a family member, or a beloved sister. She dies at a young age, just 19, in a car accident. How do you adjust to feeling cheated of what should have been many decades of time with her? Whatever the nature of the relationship—parent, child, spouse, sibling, friend, lover, business partner—the loss of a soulmate to what feels to be unfair timing reflects another facet of the Lesson of Pacing.

Through the Lesson of Pacing, you learn to view time differently. A few years or even a few decades won't change things between you and a Karmic Connection, Balance Partner, or Heartmate at the soul level where time is irrelevant. But, at the human level, feeling you didn't have enough time with someone you loved may lead you to cling too tightly to others you love, or to avoid opportunities to love again. The Lesson of Pacing in such a case is to learn the balance between honoring a loss and refusing to let go of grief. (See also Chapter 23.)

The Lesson of Pacing may also be about learning to decide when deadlines matter, and when they don't. For example, if you knew you'd only have three years with someone you loved more than anyone you'd ever known before they left you or died, would you stay in the relationship? Or would you move on in search of a Heartmate you could expect to enjoy 30 years or more with? Neither choice is right or wrong. Ask your Inner Wisdom for some insight about your motivations. Is it the emotional and spiritual depth of the relationship you're seeking with a Heartmate? Or the length in years? If you had to choose one, quality or quantity, what would you choose?

The truth is that you never know how many years you'll have with *anyone* you love. So if you want a deeply connected relationship, take time every day to communicate the depth of your feelings in some way. You only ever have Now. And Now is always a good time to tell someone you love them.

The Lesson of Pacing and Balance Partner Soulmates

Balance Partner soulmates enter your life for a season, and for a reason. They are in your life, to challenge you in positive ways, to spur you on through difficult times in your life and to support you with love and friendship. In return you do the same for them. The Lesson of Pacing with Balance Partners is often about helping each other make difficult decisions. A Balance Partner is the one who, when you express concern about returning to school after a long absence by saying, "But I'll be 42 when I finish!" responds with, "Well, won't you still be 42 if you don't do it? At least you'll be 42 with a degree."

The Lesson of Pacing among Balance Partners often features such down-to-earth advice and it comes at exactly the right time. These are the centered, grounded folks who offer practical wisdom just when you need it. You might think of Balance Partners as your Inner Wisdom manifest in human form, there to give you just the right dose of motivation to keep you moving along toward your goals.

Balance Partners don't always stay in your life for long periods. When the project you're working on together, the Lesson of Pacing you're dealing with is learned, you may go your separate ways. If you've lost touch with old friends and later tried to reconnect but noticed you don't have enough in common anymore, you understand the Lesson of Pacing: You're going at different speeds, headed in different directions.

The Lesson of Pacing and Heartmates

With romantic soulmates, the Lesson of Pacing is often about taking the time necessary to truly get to know someone you may already feel you know on a soul level. It's about patience. Slowing down the pace of an evolving relationship isn't easy when you have a burning desire to stay in close contact physically, emotionally, intellectually, and spiritually. Infatuation is a powerful force. So is sexual chemistry. But slowing down the pace allows you to savor the experience.

At a fine restaurant, you'd linger over the food and wine and the atmosphere so you could always remember the details of your special occasion. To rush through a meal someone took great care to prepare also demeans their efforts (and gives you indigestion). Savor the journey as you come to know a new romantic soulmate. Taste the relationship slowly. You don't need the emotional tummyache that will result from rushing.

The opposite issue, not moving the pace along fast enough within a Heartmate relationship can also bring the Lesson of Pacing to the forefront. If you drift along for years in a relationship with someone who doesn't share the same goals you have about whether (or when) to make a level change (moving in together, getting engaged, moving to a different city so you can be together more) ask your Inner Wisdom an important question: What's keeping you involved with this person? The comfort of the familiar? Fear that this is the best relationship you're likely to find? Plain old lack of motivation?

All things change. Nothing stays the same. Life *is* change. Is your partner trying to avoid life by refusing to decide on key points within the relationship? Are you? The Lesson of Pacing requires you to consider these deeper questions of whether you're headed in the same direction, and at what speed. Your Inner Wisdom can provide some insights about this—if you have the courage to ask.

Be sure you really want a truthful answer before you consult your Inner Wisdom. Your Inner Wisdom is the voice of your soul. It's always honest with you, even when you'd rather not face certain issues. The thing about enhancing that shining inner light, of adding soul-level experiences to your database, is that the brighter it gets, the harder it is to hide from yourself. But developing your authentic self, your Best Self, is worth the effort. The more authentic and clear you become, the better the quality of your Personal Resonance broadcast, and the higher the level of potential soulmates you'll attract.

Practical Ways to Learn the Lesson of Pacing

If you're dealing with the Lesson of Pacing, you might find it helpful to examine an important relationship using this time line exercise. Draw a line from top to bottom down the center of a page. On the left side of the page, mark the key events in your life: your birth; your graduation; your first trip out of the country; your first job; the first time you experienced grief over the death of someone you loved or a pet you cared about; when you moved away from home for the first time; marriages; divorces; children; big career changes. Make a sort of visual biography on this time line. Make notes of your emotions and your state of mind as you reflect on the events of your time line.

On the right side of the page, do the same for someone you feel is a soulmate to you, whether a relative, friend, or romantic partner. You may not know everything about the time line of their life, but put in what you can. Then compare the two time lines. Evaluate the timeline comparison chart you created to see if you have always been the leader or the follower within your relationship in terms of timing. Are you always the first to take on big life events? Or do you notice that your soulmate sets the pace and you follow? Perhaps the role of pace setter is shared, such as a runner handing off a baton in a race for someone else to carry for a while.

You may also find it helpful to extend the time line based on goals you have already in motion, big life events that are already underway. Again, compare to see whether you're a leader or a follower. Determine whether you're comfortable with your role, or whether you might like to let someone else set the pace for a while.

If you want to program your Personal Resonance to wring as much out of this precious life as possible, to be spiritually efficient so you're not creating karma you'll have to sort out later. Regularly ask your Inner Wisdom a few important questions: Are you a leader or a follower? Do you set the pace in your life, or strive to keep the pace someone else started? Then, be sure to listen and reflect on the answer.

This discussion of Lesson of Pacing isn't intended create panic that time is running out. Remember: To your soul, there's no such thing as time. Everything happens in the moment Now. Relax. You've got eternity to sort everything out.

But if you want to enjoy your human journey with some treasured soulmates and a loving Heartmate by your side, take time right Now to send out your gloriously beautiful shining Personal Resonance, that inner light that's yours alone. Tell the Universe you're ready for the adventure of a lifetime.

Chapter 22:
The Lesson
of Problem-Solving

Whatever your problem, no matter how difficult, you can release spiritual power sufficient to solve your problem. The secret is-pray and believe.

—*Norman Vincent Peale*

Whether it's a family situation, a friendship, workplace relationship, or romantic liaison, the Lesson of Problem-Solving encourages you to ensure that you're in soulmate relationships for the right reasons: soul growth and development. The Lesson of Problem-Solving brings clarity. Many times, whether it's with a Karmic Connection, a Balance Partner, or a Heartmate, a shared crisis brings you together— and keeps you involved. The Lesson of Problem-Solving requires you to reassess your life and your partnership. Maybe it's the right thing to stay connected after the problem has been solved, and maybe it's not.

The Lesson of Problem-Solving is the most practical of the Five Big Lessons, whether the issues are global and far-reaching or much more personal. Unlike the Lesson of Purpose, which is about finding out what you stand for, what your values are, what you're here on earth to do, the Lesson of Problem-Solving is a reminder to pay attention to what brings you together with others, and to periodically reassess that connection. Does it serve your higher purpose, bring out your Best Self, to be involved with this person, in this way?

The question to consider as you consult your Inner Wisdom is whether it's *who you are* at a soul level that keeps you together, or *what you're doing*. Is it the real you, your soul essence, or what you're doing for others that keeps the bond going? Finding the answer to this question requires a willingness to really look at your involvements, to squarely face the truth of What Is.

Many times the shared problem acts as the glue in the relationship. Once that problem or issue is resolved, people find that there's no deeply intimate soul-level reason to stay involved in the relationship, whether it's a family relationship, friendship, or romantic involvement. Yet people stay in disconnected, unsatisfying relationships out of habit or fear of change or a misplaced sense of responsibility.

Perhaps you know people who discovered how mismatched they were on a Personal Resonance level when the problem that brought them together was solved. Perhaps one person's health improved after a long period of illness, someone quit drinking or drugging or gambling, a struggling business became viable, the fixer-upper or brand new house was finally completed, the long road to an advanced educational degree was over, an adult parent who needed ongoing care died, or the children left home.

All of these are examples of situations in which the Lesson of Problem-Solving may be involved. What the Lesson of Problem-Solving resembles varies with the type of soulmate. Karmic Connections, Balance Partners, and Heartmates interact in different ways around the Lesson of Problem-Solving.

The Lesson of Problem-Solving and Karmic Connection Soulmates

With Karmic Connections, as you might imagine, the Lesson of Problem-Solving is common. Determining whether you want to continue to be karmically connected, or instead evolve to Balance Partners or Heartmates will help you make wiser decisions about the relationship, and on what terms and conditions you'll stay in it, or even if you'll stay in it.

For example, if the Lesson of Problem-Solving is with a family member and you finally handle what needs to be addressed—confronting someone who was in some way abusive, for example—the next issue to decide is whether you want to stay connected. And if so, on what terms—to what level?

In other words, just because you're related to someone by blood ties doesn't mean you owe them your soul. Your soul-level development is your issue, your focus, your responsibility. Your Inner Wisdom will tell you, if you ask, how to handle these Karmic Connections, and keep your integrity and your focus on becoming your Best Self. Yes, sometimes that means taking a tough-love stance by realizing that putting your own needs first makes the best sense. It offers encouragement by example.

The good news is that Karmic Connections can, and do, have the potential to evolve into bigger-better-more connections. But be spiritually efficient: Look for probability over possibility. If you come to the awareness that "she'll never change," be careful: You're programming your Personal Resonance to believe that. You'll find examples, over and over, that prove you're right. Hold open the possibility of change. Send love and healing from a safe emotional (or even geographical) distance if that's better for you.

Put yourself first when it comes to your soul growth. No one else can take those growth steps but you. This isn't to suggest you should be selfish or self-focused, but rather that you should be *soul-focused* as you make your choices about your Karmic Connection relationships. Working with your soul's needs in mind will serve you well, as it keeps you conscious of your Best Self, that divine spark, that shining light within.

Life lessons for the soul include these challenging people, certainly. But maybe, just maybe, the Lesson of Problem-Solving is also at work. Maybe it's there to remind you that, once you've dealt with the tough stuff, managed the problem as best you can, it's fine to move on. Perhaps it's even better to move on because by doing so, you leave room for the other person to grow in awareness on their own, rather than be overshadowed by you. Everyone knows there comes a time when the training wheels come off the bicycle and the child must travel under his own power.

As always, consult your Inner Wisdom about what to do with a challenging Karmic Connection soulmate. For example, if you had emotionally toxic parents or other adult role models during your childhood, you may find that as an adult, engaging with them does you more harm than good physically, emotionally, intellectually, or spiritually. In such cases, you are often better served on a soul level to step away.

Because your Personal Resonance is energetic and vibrational, you can program it to send that toxic person love, light, and healing on physical, mental, emotional, and spiritual levels. The body is necessary here on planet earth but your soul transcends it. You can love someone from a safe distance when the desire to connect is one-way or when you feel used, disconnected, or that you're still trying to please someone else.

The bottom line is this: Estrangement, even from a family member, is not necessarily a negative situation on a soul level, difficult though it is on a human one. It doesn't mean you're not trying hard enough. It means you're aware of your limits and use your free will to decide how best to proceed for your soul-level needs. Your Inner Wisdom can help you decide what's best. Ask and, more importantly, pay attention to the answers you receive, especially the repeated signs.

The Lesson of Problem-Solving and Balance Partner Soulmates

Even when people start out as Balance Partner soulmates and evolve into romantic Heartmates, through time, the Lesson of Problem-Solving can push aside deeper levels of connection if they're not attended to on a regular basis. But drifting apart can be avoided: Putting the purpose ahead of the problem is the key.

When the Lesson of Purpose and the Lesson of Problem-Solving are aligned, people are able to stay together through tough circumstances. They actually become closer on physical, emotional, intellectual, and spiritual levels. They found each other initially because they had a shared sense of purpose. Over time the challenges and problems of daily living got in the way, and pushed them apart.

Sometimes the problems or challenges they face bring them together, rather than push them away from each other. In such scenarios, both the inner drive (Lesson of Purpose) and the outer responsibility to others (Lesson of Problem-Solving) are aligned. This is understood by both parties, although not always consciously. Bringing these underlying dynamics to conscious awareness is the key to reaching and keeping level of understanding and close connection with Balance Partner soulmates.

The Lesson of Problem-Solving and Heartmates

All romantic relationships endure periods of challenge, of "same-old, same-old" stasis, and times when you wonder why you ever got together in the first place. Those lull times are the perfect opportunities to ask your Inner Wisdom for help in bringing the vibrancy, the sense of passion, the romance back into your Heartmate relationships through the Lesson of Problem-Solving. But also consider the Lesson of Purpose.

Before you give up entirely and walk away, or decide that you have no power to transform the situation, consider whether the relationship includes the Lesson of Purpose. If it does, you may find that working through the challenges with the help of your Inner Wisdom and Balance Partners for support is the better course. But sometimes, moving on, even from a Heartmate bond, is the best option for you.

If you concluded that your Inner Wisdom is calling you to move on, do so thoughtfully. Be your Best Self in interactions with your about-to-be ex, particularly if children are involved. You already know that your Personal Resonance is affected, actually programmed, by your free will, by your choices. So, choose to present yourself at as high a level as possible. Of course, you may find this a lonely road, but you can always take comfort in the knowledge that you're building a Personal Resonance that attracts others at a high level of expression.

And if you're one of those people who feels that you may never get another chance at a romantic love, remember: If you broadcast that idea via your Personal Resonance, and you'll attract others who'll help prove to you that you're right. Would you rather be right, or happy?

These days being single or being divorced once, twice, or more is common. In the United States, a little more than half of women are unmarried. Young couples marrying for the first time have a 40 percent lifetime risk of divorce. Nearly 1/3 of couples who are living together, engaged, or married for a second (or third or fourth) time have been divorced. So, let go of any stigma about being divorced, even if it's more than once. And open your pool of possible Heartmates to include all those folks who've been married before. There are lots of them. And just as with you, their motivation to be happy is probably the reason they're available now for other soulmate interactions with people who've also grown and learned along the way through the Lesson of Problem-Solving. They're people who got wise, you might say.

Practical Ways to Learn the Lesson of Problem-Solving

Gaining clarity is the best way to help you determine if you're involved a relationship that is based on the Lesson of Problem-Solving. Whatever method you use to gain clarity about your life through accessing your Inner Wisdom (and I highly recommend meditation), you can discover if you're drawn together because of the problem, the joint mission, or because you choose to be from a deeper level, the level (and lesson) of Purpose.

The question to ask your Inner Wisdom is this: Are you involved with a soulmate—whether Karmic Connection, Balance Partner, or Heartmate—primarily because you share a common problem? If your answer is "yes," it doesn't mean you won't develop other reasons to stay connected once the problem is solved. But keep in mind that some relationships are seasonal, or "reasonal." Once the situation that brought you together is handled, there's no reason to stay together. Holding yourself there only stagnates your own soul growth and development and adds static to your Personal Resonance.

You may be wondering how to tell whether you're with a soulmate because of the Lesson of Problem-Solving or the Lesson of Purpose. It's a process of discernment based on paying attention. Being conscious. If your connection comes from a deep awareness of

Purpose (what I'll call an inner drive), you'll find more reasons to stay connected than just the currently existing problem. If you discover that pretty much your interactions focus on the same set of problems—the other person's behavior or health that requires ongoing attention, for example—then you'll have to assess whether these outer drives are enough to build on.

There's no simple, straightforward, yes-or-no answer to this dilemma. Differentiating between the inner and outer drive to stay connected to certain soulmates is not easy. Even when you consult your Inner Wisdom, you may not feel you receive a clear answer. And there's no "right" answer to any question when it comes to relationships, especially whether to stay in them.

That's because you'll learn something if you stay. You'll also learn something if you leave. You've got to get back in touch with the lesson plan, with your tutor, your Inner Wisdom, to determine what you're actually learning, and whether it's the lesson you need. If you're in English class, but really should be over in math or science, you'll learn, but not the stuff that'll help you graduate to the next level.

In your journal, keep a record of your impressions over a period of time as you consider the question of whether you're involved primarily from inner Purpose or outer Problem. Attend to your feelings as you consider the question, including any physical sensations of tightness or constriction. The body knows. Write down what sensations you have and through time, you're likely to see a pattern emerge. If you think of a certain person and notice that you develop a slight headache, take note of that reaction. Pay attention to your body's responses. It won't lie to you, although you may misinterpret the cause of that discomfort, saying, "Oh it's just my allergies" when it might actually be that you're "allergic" to a particular individual. What you won't acknowledge on a mental level often will be experienced on a physical level.

Get into the habit of regularly conducting a body scan to determine where you're holding tension, feeling discomfort, or otherwise uneasy. Use your journal and periodically read through a week's or month's worth of body scan entries to see if you notice any patterns, any people who seem to trigger negative physical reactions. This process helps you learn to "hear" your Inner Wisdom through your body's cues, and works well as an adjunct or backup to meditative and other quiet-the-mind techniques.

Another way to tell if you're involved in a relationship that has problem-solving as its focus is to listen to your language, how you talk to friends about your other soulmate relationships, including your romantic ones. Listen first to your body, your "gut," but also listen to your words. Depending on the circumstances, your language about your situation and your choices will be very different. If you're in the relationship with a sense of Purpose, your voice will carry that Personal Resonance. If not, you'll sound as though you're whining. That's a clue that you're dealing with the Lesson of Problem-Solving.

Remember: Chaos is where order got its start. Chaos came first. Even when you feel overwhelmed by challenges within your relationships, you have free will to choose whether to stay involved, to change your behavior which then engenders change in the other person, or to move on.

Each day, ask for a sign of whether you're moving in the direction that best serves your soul-level growth, your divine essence, your Best Self. And if that direction includes the Lesson of Problem-Solving, know that there's an important interaction in it for you.

So, dive in. But dive in with your Inner Wisdom right there to help. Remember that you're never alone on the Soulmate Path.

Chapter 23:
Losing a Soulmate

Real love stories never have endings.

—*Richard Bach*

Death is a reality of life and yet you're never prepared to lose someone you deeply love, someone you consider a soulmate, a beloved, a Heartmate, a beshert, as it's called in Yiddish. Whether the passing is sudden and shocking, or extended over a period of time and expected, the loss of a soulmate, and particularly a Heartmate, aches, for a long time. Some would say forever.

How you look at death and what you believe about it will shape your experience of that transformation, that changed circumstance that means you are no longer living alongside your soulmate, or at least not in a physical way. If you consider life to be eternal evolution of the soul, you may view the experience of death as the next step on an eternal journey. And although you'll certainly miss the physical presence of your loved one, you won't define your experience of that person as limited to the physical world. One example is someone who's lived with a person challenged by chronic illness, whether physical or emotional. After death, those ailments that are part of living in the human body are released. You may even develop a new relationship with that soulmate after death, and sometimes it's a better one, especially with Karmic Connection soulmates with whom you've made some progress that can be continued from the other side.

Connecting with the Personal Resonance, that soul-level essence of someone who's now in the realms of spirit life, is one of the greatest blessings in my work as a psychic medium. Those who've passed on have taught me much. And among the most important lessons is this: I'm not gone as long as you remember me with love.

Those beloved soulmates on the other side remind me on a regular basis that connection between their world and ours is enhanced by focusing on it. Yes, there are random moments of mediumship, hellos from heaven. But by learning to contain and control the process through meditation, and perhaps even the study of mediumship, you can maintain an ongoing relationship in many cases.

Is this after-death relationship the same as having them here, physically present, so you can hold them close and tell them you love them? No. But if you've experienced a profound sense of presence from someone who's passed on that's so strong you can almost feel their touch (some people actually do feel their touch), smell a scent that you associate with that person, or see a sign that's impossible to misinterpret, you know it's not your imagination. It's not complicated or inappropriate grieving as some would have you believe.

In fact, this experience of feeling connected to a loved one after death is extremely common. Studies have shown that more than 2/3 of widowed people report feeling a visit from their deceased spouse within the first year. More recent studies on mediumship by several university researchers are considering what it means to our understanding of human consciousness when someone unknown to either party acting in the role of message-bearing medium (formally or informally) gathers information unknown to anyone but the deceased party (and sometimes not even them). When data is later verified, it becomes clear that at least some form of consciousness, some aspect of that soulmate, continues in some form after physical death. What that aspect is and how it interacts with our world are questions to be resolved—but that it happens is commonly known.

So, perhaps death is better seen as a transition, a transformation, a change, a birth to a new life (although one we here cannot fully understand). Seeing death as a step in the continued evolution of the soul helps people grieve in ways that respect the loss of the physical being, that honor the person, and that also continue to embrace the moment Now. To integrate the loss, both its pain and its teachings.

Of course many people, especially those who lose a young soulmate such as a son, daughter, or sibling, are challenged by such a view—that there is a soul-level teaching in that loss. They are understandably angry. They feel cheated of years together in the physical world. They struggle through each day, focusing on the loss rather than at the soul-level lessons to be learned. They cannot let go of what might have been. They can't see what opportunities to connect with and perhaps even serve others are contained within their painful loss. Death and its circumstances impact us greatly, but what we choose to do with that impact is entirely under our control.

Grief holds the power to transforms us, too. We can hold it inward, allow others to share it with us, or use it for transformation on a broader scale. Mothers Against Drunk Drivers (MADD) is a fine example that collective grief channeled into action can transform the world. As a psychic medium, I see similar examples on a regular basis, in young widows of the 9/11 disaster supporting each other emotionally, in parents of ill infants coming together to encourage research of rare diseases, or in the sibling of a teenage suicide victim choosing to pursue psychological counseling as a career.

Looking at death only as a loss can extend the grieving process. And though you may never be able to redefine the physical loss of your soulmate as a blessing, the transformed, expanded Personal Resonance you create by considering your deepest grief also as an opportunity for emotional and spiritual growth opens your heart in a way that leaves room for joyous remembrance of your loved one. An open heart leaves room for celebration of a special person who changed your life—and whose life you also changed.

Letting down the walls of grief that are built in the early stages of a loss, when keeping your grief to yourself is most common, also makes you extremely vulnerable. If you've ever known someone who seemed to sail right through the death of several close friends (which may include pets) and relatives in a short period of time, only to fall apart at a loss that seemed to be far less significant, you've witnessed the wall of grief come crashing down. You've seen someone's heart finally open to release its pain and welcome healing. You've witnessed a sort of miracle. You've seen the magnitude of someone's love and the depth of their loss at the same time.

That's a beautiful tribute to a beloved soulmate: an open heart and a willingness to learn from the experience.

Do What Works for You

By allowing your Inner Wisdom to guide you along the journey through grief you can create an experience that is uniquely yours. There is no correct way to grieve for someone who's died. There is no correct timeframe for mourning. If you know someone whom you feel began dating too soon after the loss of a spouse, for example, check your judgment. Rather than judge another's choice to reconnect romantically sooner than you feel is appropriate, see the celebration of that beloved spouse, that Heartmate in that desire to reconnect. A desire to be partnered again can be seen a tribute, a testament to a long and loving bond. You want to repeat experiences that mean a lot to you.

In fact it's quite common for those recently widowed to find comfort among people who also knew and loved their Heartmate. You probably know someone who, after decades of marriage, was widowed, and later chose a life partner among their circle of joint friends. Some would say that's an unhealthy response to grief, that by being among friends who know the individual, they're "hanging on" to the person who died. I say, see the celebration, the joy in the shared remembrance of a beloved soulmate.

If you've ever sat around the table with others, trading stories of a much-loved, long-deceased relative and laughing together, you know how much healing can be found in the joint remembrance of people you care about. Both past and present pain of grief can be healed, all from the moment Now. That's because remembering someone brings them alive again in an energetic way. Your combined Personal Resonances create a field that attracts that passed-on soulmate's Personal Resonance. What I call "field merge" is the result. That beloved soulmate is there, with you, energetically. That's why people often report having the same recollection of the same person in the same moment, even if they're chatting on the phone from long distances. Merged fields connect us across time and space, and bridge us to the worlds beyond this one.

Moving From How to Now

It's quite natural, particularly soon after someone passes, to focus on how they died. You wonder if they suffered. You think about whether the death could have been avoided. You wonder if they are angry with you that you weren't there when it happened. You play "if only" and work out fantasies of other possible outcomes. This is particularly true when the death was not from natural causes (and even more so if the death was violent). But as tough as it is to face it, the reality in the moment Now is that the *physical* presence of that individual is never going to be felt again. The *emotional* and *spiritual* presence of that person can, however, be brought into the moment. It's field merge again.

You may be familiar with the saying attributed to the teacher, Jesus: "Wherever two or more are gathered in my name, I am with you." If there's one thing I've learned through decades of connection with the Other Side, it's that this statement is true for everyone. And that truth always reminds me of that other famous teaching attributed to Jesus when he spoke of so-called miracles: "These things you can do and more." It's natural to be connected. The bonds of love are eternal.

You can open your Personal Resonance to receive the energies of those who've passed on. In the world of psychic mediumship, this is called development or unfoldment. Many mediums first become interested in ongoing development of this natural ability after the death of a soulmate, and often in childhood or adolescence. The physical death of a soulmate can help you open your heart and your mind, if you're willing to work from the level of soul, from your Personal Resonance, from your Inner Wisdom.

Whether you call it life everlasting, life on the Other Side, life after life, or something else, remember that the focus is on *life*. When you place your focus there, on life, you're likely to discover that the pain of death diminishes significantly. You can begin to see the world again as a place where joy is possible. Even after you've lost a treasured soulmate.

Creating Joyful After-Death Connections With a Soulmate

To some degree, joy is a choice. You find moments of joy by seeking them out, by choosing them, moment by moment. To create a connection around a moment of joy with a soulmate who's died, begin by focusing on something other than how they passed or how they struggled in the physical world. All that is behind them now. Focus instead on your interactions with that person. On your love for that person, your beloved friend, relative, or Heartmate (the same technique holds true for beloved pets as well). Focus on a shared adventure, on moments of lightness and laughter. Choose events to which you have a particularly strong emotional connection.

Working from the heart-center chakra, the core of your human being, where the vibration of love is best experienced, enhances your success with this reconnection technique. Open your heart. Repeat, "My heart is open to love and connection" or a similar statement whenever you feel yourself drifting away from the world of feeling into the world of thought.

As you bring those past joyful moments into the present moment Now, allow yourself to be transported into the experience again. This technique is easily learned. If you meditate, you'll find that it supports connecting with the Personal Resonance of someone who you love who's died. Connection becomes much easier when the mind is stilled. In fact, many people experience visitations from passed-on soulmates when sleeping because, for most people, that's the time when the mind is most relaxed. To hear your Inner Soulmate, the voice of your Inner Wisdom, or that of someone you love who's died, stilling the mind and clearing space for that encounter is a key step in the process. Spiritual beings and teachers come to you when you center yourself and quiet the mind. Those beings include your beloved soulmates on the Other Side. And of course, your own Inner Soulmate, your Inner Wisdom.

Use your journal to record your experiences. Writing about your grief helps you process it. Some people find it difficult to speak about their losses to anyone else. For them especially, writing can be cathartic and healing. Writing a letter to your deceased soulmate is also a technique that you'll find helps you integrate the experience. If you can't write words, draw pictures or create something else that expresses your feelings. Use your hands to speak what's in your heart.

Guidance From Passed-On Soulmates

When you lose a soulmate, you can ask that person to continue to guide you, to help you. Just as you have free will to decide what you want to do in your life, so do those who are living free of the constraints of physical bodies, in the realms of spirit. As a medium, I've found that nearly all soulmates who've passed on will help when asked, just as you help people you care about whenever you can.

Often these assistants to your Inner Wisdom (the voice of your soul and your main connection to the Source) are passed-on loved ones, your soulmates, perhaps even ancestors you never knew in life but to whom you are connected through family ties. They shift and change throughout your life. At a time when art or music interests you, your Personal Resonance broadcasts that interest.

Remember: A soulmate is someone with whom you have an affinity. As you grow and change, the soulmates from the other side that you attract also change, reflecting your growth, encouraging it further. Deceased loved ones and family members (and perhaps even people you didn't know in this life) who shared that interest or talent will be there for you. They are Balance Partners in spirit form. They are still soulmates because you share an affinity, a connection.

You can increase that support and guidance from passed-on soulmates by actively inviting it into your life. It's always there waiting, but you have to ask for guidance. This creates an interesting system because not everyone will ask for help, whether in the physical world or the spiritual ones. Those who do ask for help from spiritual (not necessarily religious) sources create a Personal Resonance far more inclusive of possibilities than those who don't. Open to possibilities is an excellent way to live life. After all, life changes every moment, and so does what's possible.

So if you're even a little bit curious, ask for guidance. For signs from your spirit guides as well as your Inner Wisdom. Test the process. Keep a record of your experiences in your journal. If it works, fine. If it doesn't, you've had one more adventure in life to add to that soul development database you're building. Either way, you win. I'm betting it'll work because if you're open to the adventure, your Personal Resonance will broadcast that fact.

Ongoing Miracles

Even though I understand how the worlds of different resonances and vibrations intertwine and connect, I'm continually astounded by the spiritual efficiency of this process. I marvel at how well it works, and also by how much better it works when you use the power of your intention, when you request help, when you are consciously aware and in the moment Now.

For example, many clients have told me that after a beloved soulmate or Heartmate died, they felt that person guiding them to other relationships, often romantic ones. Some might find such stories miraculous, but to me, they're just more evidence that the bonds of soulmates—Karmic Connections, Balance Partners, and Heartmates—are unbreakable. You never lose a soulmate. You may move on to new lessons, new adventures, but you never let go of what you learned, or the person with whom you learned it.

A young widow of age 27, Elina, told me about how in the months following her husband Jim's death, she and a friend of her husband both repeatedly dreamed of him telling each of them to consider the other as a romantic Heartmate. They were both told that Jim's love for them would only be amplified and reflected in their love for each other, which Jim was hoping to help them discover from the Other Side.

Still, neither Elina nor their friend, Matt, wanted to pursue a relationship because they felt they'd be judged by family members and friends. People would think that this was simply too strange, and too soon, that it was a way to grieve Jim, not a gift from him. Not until they were at the point of becoming romantically involved, by then more than a year later, did they tell each other about their dream communications from Jim, which were strikingly similar. He presented himself in similar clothing outside a lakeside cottage they all knew.

Today they keep Jim alive not only in their hearts, but in their lives. Both Elina and Matt continue to talk with Jim, to consult him, and to honor his presence in their lives. Now married with children, they've found that their kids routinely see "Uncle Jimmy," which only tightens the bonds among this group of soulmates. They make Jim welcome. That strong field of shared Personal Resonances is a huge part of why Jim can continue to share aspects of life with his soulmates, even from the Other Side.

Another client (Jolene) whose only child, Aaron, died just weeks before his high school graduation the first time he used heroin, felt persistently guided by him to volunteer to speak in schools about her experiences. Jolene is a very private person, and was struggling with depression over Aaron's death and feelings of responsibility, of "if only," and profound, wrenching anger at her son for leaving her at the young age of 18.

Aaron communicated to her that he didn't want to see others suffer as she had suffered because of his choice to use drugs. So as difficult as it was for her, about two years later, with Aaron's persistent encouragement from the Other Side, Jolene volunteered to speak at several area high schools. Through her speaking engagements, she met Lisa, who had had a very brief high school romance with Aaron that only lasted about two weeks—just long enough to let teenage hormonal overdrive and lust enter the picture.

Lisa had never told anyone who the father of her now 18-month-old child was because Aaron died while Lisa was just a few weeks pregnant. Aaron never even knew Lisa was carrying his baby. Lisa didn't attend his funeral because she was angry with him for breaking off their romance right after, as she saw it, "he got what he wanted."

But because she listened to the promptings of her son to talk about her experiences, Jolene was led to a granddaughter she might never have known. She has become a sort of second mother to Lisa, and longs for the day that Lisa marries and has more children she can love and nurture. And she's also transformed the lives of hundreds of people who've had the chance to hear her story, who've learned from her experiences as the mother of a son who died young, but who left quite a legacy.

Nothing replaces what you had here on earth with that special soulmate who passed on. But even though they've moved on, you never lose a soulmate. They are as real and present as your memories and your love. By listening for the gentle and repeated promptings demonstrating their ongoing presence in your life, you can continue to grow together as soulmates on different sides of the same bridge, always connected, just a thought away.

Chapter 24:
Resonating Your True
Essense

I was once afraid of people saying, 'Who does she think she is?'
Now I have the courage to stand and say, "This is who I am.

—*Oprah Winfrey*

Resonating your true essence, using your Personal Resonance to shape and transform your world, is the reason you're here on earth. You're here to live from your Best Self, to shine that divine light within and brighten the world through your presence, your essence, your Resonance. Building a relationship with your Inner Wisdom, that Inner Soulmate who wants to guide you to fruitful relationships in all areas of your life, makes that process much easier.

As you look back over the journal you've been keeping as you read *Natural-Born Soulmates,* I want you to take a moment to see how much more self-aware and empowered you are now. Just by asking questions, by seeking to better understand yourself and your relationships, you've changed your life. Please take a moment now to put down this book, close your eyes, and honor yourself for your interest in becoming your Best Self, in resonating your true divine essence, in singing the song of your soul to the world.

I hope you've learned some new ways of looking at your life through *Natural-Born Soulmates.* If you practice the principles, and pay attention to what your Inner Wisdom places before you, I know you can transform your relationships. You can't avoid it because, as you change and grow, all others around you are affected, too. The better you understand yourself, the better your ability to use your Personal Resonance in empowered and healing ways, which of course attracts empowered and healing relationships. It all starts with you.

By looking at current, past, and even future relationships you wish to attract by determining whether you're dealing with Karmic Connection, Balance Partner, or Heartmate soulmates, I hope you'll make better decisions about how to improve those relationships. What works with a more highly evolved Heartmate won't have the same effect with a Karmic Connection who represents an unfinished soul-level lesson. By understanding the three types of soulmates, you can make better strategic decisions. You can consider what your Inner Wisdom is guiding your toward. You can become more spiritually efficient.

As you look back over your journal and think about your past romantic relationships, I hope you've learned to see (and remove) blocks you may have been placing—consciously or unconsciously—in the way of your Personal Resonance. Negative self-talk and fear are the foundations of the Five Big Blocks that keep you involved in relationships, particularly romantic ones, that don't serve your best interests. But as you learn to access and apply your Inner Wisdom, you'll see that your soul-level essence, your Personal Resonance, is strong enough to break through anything you empower it to. As you strive to show your Best Self to the world, your fears become smaller and smaller as you grow larger and larger in your self-awareness.

Surrendering your agenda matters, too. Tough as it is to hold a vision of what you want to experience in your relationships, make surrendering to your Inner Wisdom a priority. It's much more efficient. Resonate what you want in terms of the concepts—*I want a loving, supportive, lasting Heartmate bond,* for example. But being too specific will only limit your success. If you're serious about attracting soulmates, let go of any preconceived notions. Let yourself be surprised by adventures your Inner Wisdom wants to bring you.

I also hope you've allowed yourself to play with the ideas I presented in this book about Now Power. Understanding that Now is all you ever have in which to make choices, that only Now has power, is a hugely freeing concept. It allows you to release the bonds of history with your soulmates. It allows you to free yourself from the lure of fantasies (and anxieties) about what might be, and puts the focus squarely on What Is. Now.

In this moment Now what do you choose for yourself? Free will is also a challenging but important concept that I hope you'll take to heart. Practice living in the Now. Learning to work from the perspective of the eternal Now empowers you in all areas of your life. Now is it—all you get. Knowing that, living that, helps you become ever and always grateful. What a powerful Personal Resonance that broadcasts. When you live in the moment, the eternal Now, you attract other soulmates who do the same.

Can you imagine your Heartmate as ever and always grateful for your presence Now? If you can't create it, you won't attract it. Use the moment Now to resonate your intentions. Choose the life you want, Now. And remember that everything in your past can be transformed, too, through Now Power. What happened is there, but transformed by how you choose to view it Now. As a lesson? As a burden? As anger? As love? It's all in your power to determine. Your use of your free will to decide, to choose moment by moment what you want your Personal Resonance to be is what transforms your life, and your relationships.

No matter how powerful you become in your ability to live in the moment, to surrender attachments, to assess soulmate situations and use your free will and your Inner Wisdom to create your life, lessons are part of the journey. Learning how to embrace those lessons, to see the Lessons of Passion, Potential, Purpose, Pacing, and Problem-Solving as opportunities to show your Best Self will also transform those very lessons. Opportunity is positive. And the opportunity to program your Personal Resonance so that you receive the most spiritually efficient lessons, so that you learn the most from all your soulmate encounters, is a gift. A gift of the spirit: yours.

I hope *Natural-Born Soulmates* has helped you. That was certainly my intention in writing it. I want to hear about your success and, yes, your challenges as you apply these ideas and concepts. I welcome you to share your soulmate stories at my Website, *DrLauren.com.*

And please, wherever you are in life, never forget you are magnificent. You are a unique and special soul. Your spirit shines brightly and is a beacon to soulmates who need your uniquely "you" vibration, your divine essence, your Personal Resonance in their lives. Open your heart and embrace who you are, all that you are.

Embrace all those soulmates who are meant to love you, too. They're all around you. Just open your heart. Welcome them to your divine essence, your soul's embrace.

Make love your Personal Resonance. Now. Always.

Resources

Dr. Lauren

www.DrLauren.com

About the Author Lauren Thibodeau, Ph.D., N.C.C., M.B.A.

The Seekers Circle

www.SeekersCircle.com

Online intuition development and self-growth community owned by the author

MENTAL HEALTH AND WELL-BEING

National Suicide Hotlines USA

suicidehotlines.com

A comprehensive list

National Board of Certified Counselors

www.nbcc.org/counselorfind2

National Association of Social Workers

www.socialworkers.org

American Psychological Association

locator.apahelpcenter.org

National Alliance on Mental Illness

www.nami.org

Online Therapy / Counseling with licensed professionals (anonymous if you prefer)

www.mytherapynet.com

RELATIONSHIP AND FAMILY COUNSELING

The Family and Marriage Counseling Directory

family-marriage-counseling.com

ALTERNATIVE & COMPLEMENTARY

American Society of Alternative Therapists

www.asat.org

National Guild of Hypnotists

www.ngh.net

DOMESTIC VIOLENCE

The National Domestic Violence Hotline

www.ndvh.org

Womenslaw.org

www.womenslaw.org

Legal information Website, including referrals and detailed protective/restraining order information, state by state

DATING VIOLENCE

www.loveisnotabuse.com

Designer Liz Claiborne's teen dating violence Website has great information for both those living with violence and their friends and family

VICTIMS OF CRIME

The National Center for Victims of Crime

www.ncvc.org

The National Center for Victims of Crime information site includes materials on domestic violence, stalking, and sexual assault

RAPE & INCEST

The Rape, Abuse & Incest National Network

www.RAINN.org

The nation's largest anti-sexual assault organization operates the National Sexual Assault Hotline and carries out programs to prevent sexual assault and, help victims.

DEATH, DYING AND BEREAVEMENT

Association for Death Education and Counseling
ADEC - The Thanatology Association

www.adec.org

Bereaved Parents of the USA (BP/USA)

www.bereavedparentsusa.org

The Compassionate Friends

www.compassionatefriends.org

Parents of Murdered Children

www.pomc.com

National Hospice & Palliative Care Organization (NHPCO)

www.nhpco.org/templates/1/homepage.cfm

Mothers Against Drunk Driving

www.madd.org

WidowNet

www.widownet.org

Pet Loss Grief Support

www.petloss.com

Index

About the Author

Lauren Thibodeau, Ph.D., N.C.C., M.B.A., is an intuitive consultant and National Certified Counselor based in Manhattan, New York. She consults internationally for an individual and corporate clientele seeking visionary insights about their situations. A professor in the accredited master's degree program of Atlantic University, a legacy of famed psychic Edgar Cayce, "Dr. Lauren" is also regularly in the media discussing soulmates, intuition, and related topics. The force behind *SeekersCircle.com*, the top ranked Website devoted to intuition and personal growth, Dr. Thibodeau has been featured on hundreds of radio and television programs, including *Psychic Investigators,* and has participated in research studies at the University of Virginia. She has been happily married for more than 20 years to her Heartmate, psychoanalytic psychotherapist Edward Thibodeau, despite the fact that he is a morning person who often wakes up singing.